## PRAISE FOR *THE TRANSPARENCY EDGE*

"Powerful insights about what everybody wants, few get, and even fewer keep. Beautifully written."

> —Gene Griessman, author of *The Words Lincoln Lived By* and *Time Tactics Of Very Successful People*

"*The Transparency Edge* provides a clear blueprint for becoming a respected leader. The principles Barbara Pagano describes will build employer/employee relationships and result in a more motivated and productive workforce. Managers and CEOs alike should read this book."

> —Cindy Ventrice, author of *Make Their Day! Employee Recognition That Works*

"A book timed perfectly for imperfect times. This is a must read for leaders. But they should do more than just read *The Transparency Edge* —they should implement its principles."

> —Donald Distasio, CEO of American Cancer Society, Eastern Division Inc.

"A powerful book by a powerful speaker! *The Transparency Edge* redefines true leadership and provides a roadmap for how leaders can succeed while working by tenets like honesty, grace, humility, and sincerity."

> —Pat Pierce, Director, Opportunity Development Center, Vanderbilt University

"This book really affirms the leadership style I aspire to and confirms principles all leaders should focus on. It is a timely and instructive guidebook for leaders in organizations who need to establish and maintain credibility."

> —James S. Beard, president of Caterpillar Financial Services Corp. and vice president of Caterpillar Inc.

"*The Transparency Edge* is the essential tool for leading, managing and advancing a workforce that has heard it all and lacks faith in the future. Nothing is as compelling to people these days as transparency, and this book offers relevant case studies and timely research into a subject that challenges even the best of leaders. In the war for talent, transparency is perhaps the most winsome trait, and *The Transparency Edge* cracks the code for those in earnest about developing this leadership survival skill."

> —Casey Hawley, author of *100+ Tactics for Office Politics* and *100+ Winning Answers to the Toughest Interview Questions*

"Relevant, refreshing, and timely! This book should be on the reading list of not only business leaders, but every MBA student and management professor."

> —Dr. Liz Thach, professor of Management, Sonoma State University School of Business & Economics

"Barbara Pagano is a great coach. *The Transparency Edge* not only can help you become a better leader, it can help you coach others so that they become better leaders."

> —Marshall Goldsmith, listed in *The Wall Street Journal* as one of the nation's "top 10" executive educators and author/editor of 16 books on leadership

"Finally, a book about leadership that does more than just tell us to "develop a vision." And what it tells us will turn the field of leadership, rightfully so, on its head! The old leader behaviors of bravado, charisma, and arrogance gave us debacles like Enron, Worldcom, and Arthur Andersen. The transparent leader offers a set of new, and ultimately more prosperous and enduring, leader behaviors. Things like rigorous honesty, vulnerability, reasonability, and humility. Ultimately this book proves what we've suspected all along, that authenticity is far more powerful than authority."

> —Bill Treasurer, author of *Right Risk*, and founder of Giant Leap Consulting

"While many of today's business leaders are reeling from the ravages of ethics inquiries at home and abroad, the impact of low morale, and the struggles of managing discontinuous change, a few smart executives understand that the benefits of their own loyalty to others, a clear and open style, and personal vulnerability are personal attributes which drop benefits right to the business bottom line! These leaders are building and sustaining themselves plus their organizations by honing their own Transparency Edge. Others would be well served to do so, too."

> —Ray Capp, author of *When You Mean Business About Yourself*, CEO of ConduIT Corporation, and former EVP of Thomas Nelson Publishers and COO of Ingram Entertainment

"Barbara Pagano has reached beyond 'Emotional Intelligence' into something even more substantive—leadership transparency. Her insights are brilliant, and her leadership prescription, if followed, will revitalize your company and recharge its culture."

> —Dr. Jim Harris, author of *Leadership at the Top* and *Finding and Keeping Great Employees*

"One of the foundations of my professional career has been to never stop learning—and *The Transparency Edge* is a powerful learning instrument for managers at any level."

> —Gary Strack, CEO, Boca Raton Community Hospital

"Wonder why your people are half-hearted in their commitment to your ideas? Want to know what stands between you and significantly greater leadership influence? Read this book. Want more than knowledge? Practice what Barbara Pagano teaches in this essential volume and your leadership effectiveness will soar."

> —Joseph Grenny, co-author of *Crucial Conversations: Tools for Talking When Stakes are High*

"*The Transparency Edge* goes to the heart of what real leadership is all about. It offers a practical guide to anyone ready to take the first step toward meaningful organizational change and any leader wishing to produce profound results."

> —William E. Troutt, president of Rhodes College

"Having consulted with businesses and corporations in their recruitment and retention strategy for over 25 years, I have noted that most people don't leave companies because of money or a 'better opportunity'...they leave because their manager lacked the leadership skills and credibility to motivate others to follow, usually promoting a clandestine or Byzantine environment. As Barbara Pagano so aptly delivers, transparency is the trend to stay for tomorrow's leaders."

> —Margot King, radio talk show host and producer of "Job Talk" and founder and CEO of Fork in the Road Communications

"As a Small Business Investment Company, we invest millions of dollars in businesses. *The Transparency Edge* defines "the new test" for measuring good talent in which to invest, and it gives us a tool to not only evaluate but to educate our portfolio CEOs."

> —Whitney Johns Martin, CEO, chair and co-founder of Capital Across America, Inc.

"The credibility that comes from the very process of striving for transparency is part of building leadership and teaming mastery. I've worked with Barbara, so I know first-hand that her concepts and her process are powerful and effective."

> —Ken Denman, president and CEO, iPass, Inc.

"When I was with Coca-Cola, I worked with Barbara Pagano in putting together the initial strategies of driving an integrated supply management approach across the business system (Coca-Cola Company and its bottlers worldwide). We were very successful in driving implementation, and transparency was a key enabler. Barbara's concepts are on target and very much in line with my personal beliefs and how I have always tried to lead. Read her book and learn how to build credibility through transparency—it is essential for sustainable business success."

> —Carl K. Kooyoomjian, executive vice president, Technical Affairs and Worldwide Operations, Revlon Inc.

"If you're trying to build credibility, this book shows you how to do it. It is compelling and insightful on a tough and timely topic."

> —R. Clayton McWhorter, chairman of Clayton Associates, founder and chairman of LifeTrust America, former chairman and CEO of HealthTrust, and former chairman of HCA

"Pagano, you hit the nail right on the head. *The Transparency Edge* embraces the key ingredient for organizational and individual success. Super job!"

> —Keith Harrell, author of *Attitude Is Everything*

"As the world changes, so must business leaders push themselves to change the way they run their companies. While still a rarity, transparent leadership—as defined in *The Transparency Edge*—is fast becoming a common goal for leaders who want to succeed and the new standard by which they are measured by their followers."

> —Lee Larsen, regional vice president, Rocky Mountain Region, and Denver market manager, Clear Channel Communications, Inc.

"Dynamic, inspiring, and real-world! Truly a must-read for every person who wants to know how to incorporate the synergy of servant leadership, genuine authenticity, and credibility in their lives."

> —Linda Wind, CEO and president, Possible Woman Enterprises, Inc., and chair, Possible Woman Foundation International

"Leadership confidence is a new item on the balance sheet, written in 'invisible ink.' You may not be able to see it but you know when it is missing. How do leaders earn credibility and the confidence of their constituents? Read *The Transparency Edge* to find out."

> —Molly Breazeale, global talent developer, ING Americas

"In a culture where business practices push the ethical envelope, anger is fashionable, and self-composure is a lost art, Barbara Pagano not only outlines better options for workplace behavior, she offers a roadmap for getting there as well. Indeed, transparency can transform, if one is willing to do the work."

—C. Leslie Charles, author of *Why Is Everyone So Cranky?*

"To engage, retain and develop talent calls for leaders to exhibit the critical personal dimensions described by the authors. Any organization that does not have 'transparency' on their leadership competency list will want to amend it immediately after reading this highly readable book."

—Dr. Beverly Kaye, founder and CEO of Career Systems International and co-author of *Love'Em or Lose 'Em: Getting Good People to Stay* and *Love It, Don't Leave It: 26 Ways to Get What You Want at Work*

# The Transparency Edge

How Credibility Can Make
or Break You in Business

Barbara Pagano

*and Elizabeth Pagano*

........................................................................................................

McGraw-Hill

New York   Chicago   San Francisco   Lisbon
London   Madrid   Mexico City   Milan
New Delhi   San Juan   Seoul
Singapore   Sydney   Toronto

First McGraw-Hill paperback edition published 2005.

1 2 3 4 5 6 7 8 9 0   AGM/AGM   0 9 8 7 6 5 4 3 (HC)
1 2 3 4 5 6 7 8 9 0   FGR/FGR   0 9 8 7 6 5 (PBK)

ISBN 0-07-142254-4 (HC)
ISBN 0-07-145884-0 (PBK)

McGraw-Hill books are available at special discounts to use as premiums and sales promotions, or for use in corporate training programs. For more information, please write to the Director of Special Sales, Professional Publishing, McGraw-Hill, Two Penn Plaza, New York, NY 10121-2298. Or contact your local bookstore.

**Library of Congress Cataloging-in-Publication Data**

Pagano, Barbara.
    The transparency edge : how credibility can make or break you in business / By Barbara Pagano, Elizabeth Pagano.
        p.   cm.
      ISBN 0-07-142254-4 (alk. paper)
      1. Business eithics.   2. Leadership—Moral and ethical aspects.   I. Title.

HF5387.P34   2004
658.4'092—dc21                                                    2003011376

*To Junior E. Stapleton, father and grandfather,*
*for his fortitude and love of growing things.*

# Contents

# Foreword

For the last four years I have been the unwitting but willing participant in what may prove to be the largest natural organizational change experiment ever conducted. I call this the FISH! Phenomenon. All over the world men and women have been stimulated by the image of a dozen fish mongers drawing on the old wisdom we call the FISH! Philosophy, to create a workplace so amazing that people flock from around the globe just to experience the energy.

And the response of these unlikely change agents who visit the market in books, films and in person, has been to do things once thought impossible or improbable at best. They have redefined the field of organizational change by provoking massive cultural shifts in hundreds of organizations from the inside out, fueled with natural energy and little else.

While the rules of change and motivation are being rewritten, the role of leadership is also under considerable scrutiny. If large scale changes can be fomented from within an organization, as well as from the top, what does this say about the role of leadership? It is that question that brings me directly to the book you have just started reading.

We have learned that a change which requires individual commitment to succeed can be initiated anywhere in the organization but is only fueled by natural energy. And this natural energy is inspired and maintained by certain kinds of leaders; leaders who practice what Barbara Pagano calls *transparent leadership*. The transparent leaders are those who build credibility through overwhelming honesty, real vulnerability, fierce conversations, keeping commitments, grace, humility, composure and sincere cheerleading. It is with the support of transparent leaders that we are able to build and sustain a workplace that is both productive and deeply human.

In the rich book that follows, Pagano outlines the elements of transparent leadership, supplies powerful examples for each and then clarifies each element down with behavioral anchors that are immediately useful to anyone who understands you don't have to be bad to get better at leadership. I strongly endorse this book's content and its spirit.

—Stephen C. Lundin Ph.D.
author of *FISH!*, *FISH! Tales* and *FISH! Sticks*

# Acknowledgments

Prior to writing this book, the two of us sailed a 43-foot boat more than 2,000 miles for five months. Little did we know how apt a prerequisite that journey was for writing this book. The hard work, triumphs, and long nights required in sailing a small boat alone foreshadowed our writing experience. We met both challenges successfully but certainly not with our strength alone. We owe a debt of gratitude to people who helped along the way as well as those who cheered us on.

Laureen Rowland, our agent, was like a half moon in a dark night sky, lighting our way, encouraging our work, and believing in what could be. She consistently meets all nine expectations of credibility. She is phenomenal.

Our editor, Mary Glenn, upped the ante on our ideas and created a vision we likely would have never found. She and the rest of the McGraw-Hill team, including Daina Penikas and Ed Chupak, were upbeat and always helpful.

Jennifer Taylor and Karen Walker at Assessment Plus were early believers in this project, and without their generosity of time, talents, and resources, this book would not be so rich. We left every meeting with them inspired. Gabe Hudson's expertise made the data reader friendly.

We emailed certain people often and asked, "Can you help us?" Bud Carter, Susan Wise, Susan Gordon, Cindy Solomon, and Linda Wind opened their vast networks and gave us entrées to leaders whose stories enriched this book. We're sure they had other important things to do and so we are very grateful.

We especially thank Cecil Murphey, Renee Grant-Williams, Sandra Ford Walston, and Marti Barletta for taking the time to share their experiences.

Thank you to those leaders who gave us their confidence and willingly shared their stories, both openly and anonymously.

We also acknowledge each other. This book is a result of our combined talents, differences, and unique perspectives.

.............................................................

An oval ring of stainless steel engraved, "Never, Never, Never Give Up"—a gift from Deanna Berg—arrived midway through this project and glowed on my desk at dawn, keeping me focused. Everyone should have a friend so special.

My colleagues, Susan Wise, Casey Hawley, Yvonne Weinhaus, and Connie Glaser, had reserves of encouragement when mine were low. Thanks to Richard Weylman for his suggestions on an early version of the manuscript and for the dock space at Miller's Marina.

My first opportunity as a leadership consultant was at Sara Lee, after Chess Chesser came from the back of a college classroom and said, "I'd like you to come to our company." It was a career changing moment, and I am grateful.

Kevin Hummel, Tom Heinselman, and Meg Burns, successful consultants all, share not only their talents but also opportunities to partner.

No one could have predicted a friendship for over thirty years between a girl from eastern Kentucky and a genuine New Yorker, but my life is rich because of Janice Caruso, who never fails to offer sound advice and support. I love her laughter.

Thanks to my husband, Herb Ludwig, who donned his tux and went to holiday parties alone, because I was "on a roll" with my writing. He has forever given me freedom along with his love.

—Barbara Pagano
*Pensacola, Florida*
*July 2003*

I have deep respect and appreciation for my teacher, partner, and co-captain, Barbara Pagano, who also happens to be my mother. She's been my coach—fee waived—for more than three decades.

Some from my past who inspired or taught me: Mary Hance, Tonnya Kennedy, Pat Embry, and especially Tim Tanton.

My dear friends, Dr. Gene Battles and Geoff Sobeck, were not only supportive company but filled my condo with tulips in the dead of an isolating winter. Betty Brooks is an adopted grandmother, and I thank her for cheering me on and caring for Smyrna, the cat. Special appreciation goes to Casey Hawley, for her wisdom and generous spirit. And for their constant interest and friendship, thanks to: Tammy Boland, Sam McPherson, Ingrid Baker, Tisa McMackin, Debi Bembenek, Beth Chaplin, Bruce Meyer, and my NAPC book club.

Love and thanks to Jerry Jordan for his care and laughter.

Herb Ludwig's support and encouragement, in everything I've ever done, have never waned. No stepfather could be a better friend.

I thank Cynthia Pagano for her good heart.

And to my father, Ray Pagano: thank you for your example of hard work and entrepreneurship and for the pride in your eyes.

—Elizabeth Pagano
*Atlanta, Georgia*
*July 2003*

# CHAPTER 1

# Leadership Transparency That Builds Credibility

*You can violate those rules [of humility and integrity] for a season, but the trap door will eventually open up. And you'll fall through.*

—James Blanchard, CEO OF SYNOVUS,
#9 ON *FORTUNE*'S "100 BEST COMPANIES
TO WORK FOR IN AMERICA"

Enron, WorldCom, Arthur Andersen, and Martha Stewart may have been just a few bad apples that fell from the tree, but the rest of the bunch must now suffer the critical eye of inspection. Like it or not, the recent swath of corporate and political scandals blasted the public's "leader as hero" viewpoint, if one ever existed, and our ethical threshold has become much less accommodating to greed and questionable business practices. There has been a basic shift in what it means to be a true leader. While market performance may still be king, the board of directors is now more apt to show the door to a chief executive officer (CEO) who may have just the touch in increasing stock value but has somehow developed a reputation that smacks of something less than ethical. Successful leadership is now a marriage of equal partners—performance and credibility.

In reaction to this shift, companies are perhaps more zealous in their search for ways to put some honor back in business. As the search continues, a word has begun to pop up more and more in management circles: *transparency*. A transparent method of operation, some believe, may just be business's *weapon of mass destruction* in the war on corruption.

The concept of transparency—a sort of "what you see is what you get" code of conduct—is a well-developed model from a financial governance standpoint; full financial disclosure is an essential part of securities laws. Yet transparency is in a more adolescent stage as it applies to management and, more specifically, leaders. Indeed, as the need for transparency has become apparent and more organizations have begun calling for it so as to be more credible to their customers, investors, and employees, leaders have been left to wonder: What exactly does it mean to me? How do I become a transparent leader? The most astute leader will ask a question that is perhaps most relevant: How do I practice transparency in a way that maintains or builds credibility?

Lest we get hitched to the wagon of yet another management fad and are somehow led to believe that transparency is next to godliness, one thing should be made clear: Transparency alone will not result in a perception of credibility any more than the open-book philosophy of the 1990s did. Transparency by itself is a simplistic prescription.

Practiced in ways that show or maintain respect and concern both for the individual and for the common good, however, transparency can lead to amazing things. Organizations benefit from a more efficient process of decision making and tactical execution as players are more informed, operations speed up, and problems are identified more readily along the way. Leaders build trust and experience more finely tuned collaboration with their peers and followers. And both the organization as a whole and the individual leader are perceived as having a higher level of credibility.

Another crucial element of transparency that leads to credibility is figuring out just how open to be—just how much to hang on the line for all to see—for while there can be too little transparency, there also can be too much. And who determines the optimal level? The leaders themselves.

# CREDIBILITY THROUGH RESPONSIBLE TRANSPARENCY

When transparency is employed without a keen understanding of the potential effects of revealed information, it can be unfair and irresponsible both to the organization and to its individual members. Leaders have to have a firm finger on the pulse of their organization and its culture, knowing people's capacity to absorb information and anticipating how it might be interpreted and used. It is in part an artful use of intuition. Yet there are practical guidelines that can help leaders wrestle with decisions around transparency.

Both transparency and credibility imply a relationship of two or more people. A person cannot be transparent unless he or she has someone to be transparent to. Similarly, a person's level of credibility is based on the perception of another person—whether you think you are credible ultimately says little about your reputation, since your reputation is determined by what others think of you. Both transparency and credibility are demonstrated through actions.

This is good news for the leader trying to master transparency while building credibility because both can be achieved through specific behaviors. By adhering to the following nine behaviors, a leader fulfills the expectations of credibility, and these behaviors are prescriptions that should play an important role in determining how to be transparent.

## Being Overwhelmingly Honest

While truth telling in organizations can be complicated and messy, honesty must be an unbroken guiding principle, the hub on the leadership wheel. And it must be visibly demonstrated through actions and decisions, or trust and credibility will not exist. When transparent leaders decide not to share certain information with their followers—perhaps because they do not yet have all the pieces or because, for whatever reason, they are unable to tell—the unbreakable principle of honesty requires them to say so: "I can't tell you that right now, but here's what I can say." Overwhelming honesty should be delivered with respect and concern for others. Followers should not be left to wonder about hidden agendas. When leaders drive this core value down through their team, not only is trust built, but another fantastic result also can occur—followers become tolerant of not having all the facts.

### Gathering Intelligence

Asking others for their opinions about something conveys respect and shows others that you value them. It also promotes transparency as a reciprocal agreement. When leaders ask for feedback about their own performance and discover how others perceive them, they are better able to align their intentions with reality and develop a plan for improvement. In order to learn and grow, we must have self-awareness, which, ironically, requires input from others.

### Being Composed

Effective and admirable leadership requires composure. Challenges, stressors, and obstacles are inherent in any organization and in any leader's path; how leaders conduct themselves during the good times and the bad can be indicative of their character, competence, and ultimately, their credibility. While the call for transparency that builds credibility urges leaders to reveal their true opinions and emotions regarding relevant business issues, it does not allow for leaders to irresponsibly let it all hang out. Followers expect their leaders to be composed. And they are always watching. Also, a certain level of predictability builds trust.

### Letting Your Guard Down

Leaders who keep in mind the spirit of authenticity while working hard to create meaningful connections with their followers, demonstrating sincerity of being and revealing personal information that adds value to the context of work, will be practicing an important part of leadership transparency that builds credibility. Doing so, however, requires a certain level of maturity and self-awareness and a heightened sense of how people might perceive, dissect, and disseminate the information that you reveal. And because authenticity or personal transparency ultimately describes the quality of a relationship, leaders must create opportunities in which to engage with their followers, allowing the followers to know them.

## Keeping Promises

When leaders match their words and actions and do what they say they will do, those leaders place a high value on their commitments. Promise keeping in leadership is not always clear-cut. Sometimes leaders are forced to reconsider promises and disappoint followers. Those are the times when transparency is particularly important because followers who understand the reasoning behind broken promises may be more accepting of the consequences.

## Properly Handling Mistakes

How you handle mistakes actually may be more important than getting things right the first time. Even with its inherent risks—such as appearing weak, incompetent, or otherwise less than perfect—confessing mistakes signals courage, accountability, and humility. Indeed, mistakes are an opportunity to visibly demonstrate a commitment to honesty.

## Delivering Bad News Well

Delivering bad news can be tricky business, yet doing it well is an essential part of leadership transparency that builds credibility. When sensitive, controversial, or potentially hurtful information is not delivered well, people can feel a sense of betrayal, anger, and indignation. Trust is destroyed and relationships suffer. For most leaders, delivering bad news is hard, and some even opt for silence. Those on the receiving end usually appreciate bad news that is delivered promptly and with honesty, directness, care, and concern.

## Avoiding Destructive Comments

Leadership that builds and maintains credibility requires transparent communication that shows the highest respect for people. Language that divides or is otherwise destructive can undermine the whole reasoning behind leadership transparency—to improve relationships, increase trust, and build a credible reputation. Leaders must model and reward language that does not employ inappropriate blame or criticism, us-versus-them attitudes, or talking down.

## Showing Others That You Care

In order for leaders to be successful at influencing and motivating people, their followers must have a solid answer to the question: Do you care about me? Leaders must visibly show their followers that, yes, they do care, and this is done by developing the followers, recognizing them, and seeking to know and understand them. While showing value for employees has lasting, bottom-line benefits in morale, quality, and productivity, a leader should not be motivated to demonstrate care and value for the organization's benefit alone. Such a narrow view undermines the formula and ultimately devalues the individual players in an organization. True leadership is built on a kind of social contract that says, "Follow me, and I promise that I will help you succeed." When this contract is not honored, the motivation behind a leader's strategy of transparency is put into question, and followers are led to wonder about hidden agendas.

So how do these behaviors play out in the real world? Consider Brenda Rivers, CEO of Andavo Travel, a $70 million travel company based in Denver. Not long after Rivers purchased the company in 1991, when it was a $15 million leisure agency, the travel industry met serious challenges in commission cuts from airlines and the Internet, which allowed consumers to easily bypass travel agencies. Rivers and her 98 employees managed to reinvent their business model and continue growing while many agencies in the industry were staving off starvation. Then came September 11, 2001, and suddenly travel was the last thing on Americans' minds. "Nothing could have prepared us for 9/11," Rivers said. "It had a profound impact on us and shook the very foundation of our industry."

Tens of thousands of people were laid off in the industry—including employees from major airlines, call centers, and agencies—and Rivers also could have downsized her staff and maybe even dusted off her law degree, readying herself for better opportunities. Instead, no Andavo employees were laid off, and the year following 9/11 was the company's best year ever in revenues and profit margins.

How did Andavo achieve such success in the face of a catalog of bumpy changes and a roiling marketplace? The answer is in part due to sound business strategy, because Andavo, as already mentioned, had prepared itself for industry shifts by changing from a traditional agency to an Internet-based travel company that also offers traditional personalized service. However, another key element to Andavo's success was Rivers, who captained her crew with a clear commitment to transparency, practiced in ways that only a credible leader would.

## A TRANSPARENT LEADER
## IN UNCERTAIN TIMES

The weeks that followed the tragedies of September 11 were frantic for Andavo employees. The airlines were canceling most flights, and because the airlines' telephone lines were jammed, Andavo became their "mouthpiece," fielding client questions about the location of their executives and how to get them home. Andavo offered full refunds, including all fees that are normally nonrefundable, and did not charge for ticket refunds. "It seemed the right thing to do," Rivers said. Yet doing so would cost Rivers dearly.

At the end of a 2-week blur was what Rivers now refers to as "the moment in the kitchen." In the employee break room, Andavo's controller informed Rivers that there was more money going out the door than coming in. At the current rate, Andavo would have to close its doors by the end of the year. "The future flashed in front of me," Rivers recalled. "If we were losing that much money, the obvious solution was massive layoffs. But there was a voice inside me saying there had to be another way." After a lot of thought and consideration, Rivers decided how to go forward.

### She Was Overwhelmingly Honest

A week after the conversation with her controller in the kitchen, Rivers shared the bleak financial picture with all her employees. Most were gathered in Andavo's conference room, and others were listening via a telephone conference. Rivers told them that in order to survive even for the next couple of months, more than a third of them would need to be laid off. Yet, she added, she really did not want to see that happen. The only other way, Rivers explained, was to creep along with deep cuts in expenses.

### She Asked for Their Feedback

"Help me make this decision," Rivers told Andavo employees. While employees huddled in groups and began looking at cash flow, Rivers left for the airport, headed for the San Francisco office. When she landed in California, she checked her voice mail and received a message from her employees: They wanted to stay, and to do so, they would take a 10 percent pay cut, slash expenses, and work like hell. While Andavo employees took these kinds of measures in trying to make things work, Rivers would not lay off anyone. Her promise would be a hard one to keep.

### She Remained Composed

Over the weeks that followed, Rivers kept a calm presence, setting the pace and keeping everyone focused on the plan. "She's a very real person. She shows that she understands what people are going through, and she shows her emotions, but she does so in a calm way that doesn't get everyone panicked," one employee said.

### She Let Her Guard Down

Sometimes during the crisis period, at the end of a torturously long day, Rivers would reveal her humanness to her direct reports, particularly her chief accounting officer (CAO) and her chief operations officer (COO), Sharolyn Clark. Clark vividly remembers one evening when Rivers came into her office and slumped down on the couch. "Suddenly this very attractive woman with the most beautiful skin in the world looked like she had aged 20 years in one day. It shocked me to see her like that." Rivers shared that she had not been sleeping at nights and said that there were days when she was physically ill and did not know whether she would make it through. "When I got home that night, I practically shook," Clark said. "I realized this wasn't a big corporation with huge, deep pockets like the one I'd come from. This was a person's livelihood." Clark always felt that she had "treated the money like it was important," but after that conversation with Rivers, Clark became a "bulldog" about going after companies that owed Andavo money.

### She Kept Her Promise

Even with severe belt tightening, the expectation of a new piece of business a few months down the road, and a fully committed workforce, financial ends were not meeting, and cash was drying up. In November—almost 2 months after the terrorist attacks—Andavo could not meet its payroll. Tapping into a bank line of credit was not an option; when Andavo's credit line had come up for renewal in September, the bank backed out, saying that the travel industry was no longer viable. Determined to keep her promise to Andavo employees, Rivers funded the business with several hundred thousand dollars from her personal assets, borrowing from her retirement fund, and taking second mortgages on real estate investments.

### She Delivered Bad News

Meanwhile, the California office was feeling neglected. While Rivers spent one full week a month at their office, the 20-person team wanted more; they wanted a full-time person to manage them. At first, Rivers had to tell them that a manager's salary simply was not in the budget and that they would have to manage as a team for a while. When it became clear that that approach was not working, Rivers hired a manager. Six months later, Rivers had to deliver more bad news. The new manager was not doing the job and had to be terminated.

### She Admitted Her Mistakes

"It would have been easy to just say she was a bad manager, but she wasn't," Rivers told the group the next morning. "I made a hiring mistake." Calling it an "error in judgment," Rivers said that she was sorry but that she could not afford to hire another manager. She encouraged the group to work out their differences and try the team approach again. "You guys can make this work. I know you can."

### She Avoided Destructive Comments

The different branches and divisions within Andavo all suffered losses during the first quarter after 9/11, but some—depending on their business mix (in this industry, the ratio of leisure versus business travelers)—suffered far deeper losses than others. In fact, some divisions of Andavo were "carrying" others for a while. To have revealed this information to all Andavo employees in her regular quarterly report, Rivers said, would have been irresponsible. Such "finger pointing" might have stirred animosity and "us-versus-them" attitudes instead of Andavo's usual team orientation. In her report, Rivers did not break out financials into the different divisions but shared information about the company as a whole.

### She Showed That She Valued Others

Fast forward to the first anniversary of September 11. Rivers asked Andavo employees to gather in the conference room, and they all stood in a circle and held hands during a moment of silence. Rivers thanked them for pulling together during the past year and reminded them how much they had to be proud of. Andavo employees had been encouraged to feel proud all year long; even though the budget was unusually tight, Rivers had continued to show appreciation. Instead of a holiday party at a fancy restaurant, the team gathered at an Andavo executive's home for a simple meal and an exchange of "white elephant" gifts (something one has but is willing to give away). Every employee also received a personalized, handwritten note from Rivers, thanking each for his or her individual and unique contribution to Andavo's success.

Indeed, Andavo had weathered the storm and came out with 25 percent revenue growth, not one lost customer, and no layoffs. Workers in the San Francisco office pulled together and, after several months, told Rivers that they would not need a manager after all. And with Andavo back on track, Rivers even had her nest egg back.

# HOW THESE NINE EXPECTATIONS WERE DETERMINED

Through more than 20 years in leadership development and executive coaching, I have learned that a leader does not have to excel in all 86 indicators on a leadership assessment tool to get the most from his or her people. If a leader is top-notch in all nine of the behaviors I have outlined, people usually will work just as hard for him or her—indeed sometimes harder—despite that leader's lack of visionary skills or strategic planning abilities.

Although I have gained a lot of knowledge directly from the near 3,000 leaders I have coached, I have perhaps learned the most from those leaders' followers, peers, and bosses. *What does this leader do that's particularly effective? What could he or she improve? What's getting in his or her way of being great?* No one would argue with the fact that great leaders need vision, competence, and determination. What distinguished the outstanding leaders, however, the ones who made people feel so much passion for their work, the ones whose people were able to say, "I'd go to hell and back for my boss," always came back to the nine behaviors of credibility.

I discovered that what people expect from leaders is usually rooted in the basic interpersonal operation of the leader-follower relationship, where personal connections are made through trust, reliability, care, and appreciation. Once this platform was built well and maintained, leaders could deliver the rest of what they had to offer—their talents—and business flourished. However, when leaders did not succeed in building this platform by meeting the nine expectations, the connection with followers was weak, and there was little chance to move to a higher level of effectiveness and success. Many leaders I have worked with, on recognizing their faulty platform, took action to improve. They strengthened their credibility, made powerful connections with people, and were more effective. Their stories are in this book.

The people who work for and with the CEOs, senior managers, and entrepreneurs I have coached have made it clear that meeting these nine expectations is a basic requirement for successful working relationships and that skipping over these basics and working on something else instead—becoming a masterful change agent or a more powerful orator, for example—will be like rearranging the deck chairs on the *Titanic*. This means that I tell leaders: "If you want to work on listening skills while you have a reputation for straying from the truth, well, it's not going to work." Or "No matter how you improve your delegation skills, you still won't be effective if your followers don't see you as someone who keeps his or her promises."

I have surveyed more than 2300 executives, and 99 percent of the respondents say that credibility is more important than ever before. And if you had it and then lost it, 92 percent say that it would be very difficult to gain it back. Certainly the tarnished reputations and lost careers of politicians, corporate executives, and priests have reminded us how fragile credibility can be.

Over the years, I have partnered in various leadership projects with Kim Jackson, chairman of Assessment Plus. Since 1984, Assessment Plus (www.assessmentplus.com) has provided survey-related services to both large and small corporations, including Oracle, BMW, Sun Microsystems, Coca-Cola Enterprises, Inc., Merck, Pfizer, Norrell, Verizon, and Cox Communications. Services include organizational and individual (360-degree feedback) assessments, survey development and design, administration, data collection, report design and production, coaching, and consulting. Two of Assessment Plus's officers who are also experienced executive coaches—Jennifer Taylor, president, and Dr. Karen Walker, director of client solutions—share the ideas behind this book and gave access to a vast database of thousands of executives who have participated in surveys. Those data are included throughout this book and affirm the importance of the nine behaviors to leadership success. Also with the help of Taylor and Walker and the staff at Assessment Plus, I have developed a 360-degree leadership assessment—*Transparency Edge 360*™—specifically tied to the nine behaviors that are already being used in corporations and businesses.

## GOING FORWARD

A July 2002 Gallup poll indicated that more than 7 in 10 Americans distrust CEOs of large corporations and nearly 8 in 10 believe that top executives of large companies will take "improper actions" to help themselves at the expense of their companies (*USA Today*/CNN/Gallup Poll, 7/16/2002). The demand for transparent, credible leadership is fast becoming a priority, and those who do not measure up will not be tolerated.

As organizations seek to be more credible and implement strategies to become more transparent, there likely will be some discomfort, especially for those responsible for being more transparent. Companies and leaders will be forced to address their undesirable areas and deficiencies if the fog is removed. Yet in the clearing of these awkward stages of building a more transparent operation are benefits for both the organization and its leaders—increased trust, effective collaboration, and overall better organizational health. And when people are allowed to see those undesirables and deficiencies, some likely will try to help to turn them around.

In turning leadership around, in helping organizations become more transparent and always credible, leaders not only must develop an intuitive sense of transparency's optimal level, but they also must fulfill the nine expected behaviors of credibility. If leaders hone this basic platform with their peers and followers and build a reputation marked by rock-solid credibility, they sometimes will be excused from the rigorous procedures of transparency, no longer having to account for every action and reasoning. Trust will have returned. And those leaders will experience the power that comes from sharing knowledge—instead of holding onto it—and the success that comes when they are always preceded by a credible reputation.

# CHAPTER 2

# Be Overwhelmingly Honest

*What upsets me is not that you*
*lied to me, but that from now on*
*I can no longer believe you.*

—Friedrich Nietzsche,
GERMAN PHILOSOPHER

Harriette Watkins, an officer for an Atlanta-based utility company, is committed to being honest even though honesty doesn't always pay. This commitment was put to the test a few years ago, when Watkins was working as an internal organizational development consultant for another company. In this role, Watkins acted as a facilitator in a meeting of six senior-level executives who were wrestling with how to get buy-in from the company's employees on tightening budgets and cutting expenses.

"There were a number of economic factors, including a down economy, that required the company to really go lean, and yet a vast number of employees didn't understand that belt-tightening was necessary," Watkins said.

As the facilitator in this meeting, Watkins worked to ensure that the group stayed focused on the topic at hand, but otherwise, she did not intervene in the conversation. Then the executive vice president who was hosting the meeting said to Watkins, "You probably have a better pulse on the employees since you interact with them more than we do. So what is going on? Why don't they seem to believe that we have to be lean?"

Watkins was concerned about being brought into the conversation and where it might lead. And yet she felt she must answer the question honestly. "Well, leadership has to be modeled, and if employees are sensing that the behavior is not being captured at the top, then it won't trickle down."

The executive vice president wanted more. "Can you give us an example of that?"

In fact, an example of the company's leadership not modeling a more frugal mindset was fresh in Watkins' memory. Two weeks earlier, a senior executive had traveled in the company's helicopter to a meeting that was held less than 60 miles away. At that meeting, an announcement was made to all the employees that a particular car needed to be moved to make way for the helicopter landing. Watkins overheard employees' comments indicating they believed the executive was being extravagant by using an expensive helicopter instead of simply driving 60 miles.

To relay this example to the senior executives at the meeting she was now facilitating would be risky. "I'm sitting there with all officers, and that's an officer perk," Watkins said. "By telling that example, I may have been really stepping on their toes."

She told it anyway, without naming the particular executive who had used the helicopter and who happened to be present at the meeting Watkins was facilitating. Yet even though she didn't name him, everyone knew he was the one she spoke of, and he was furious with her. After the meeting, he barred Watkins from doing any work within his part of the organization.

While Watkins suffered the negative consequences of her honesty, she also saw the benefits, among them an increased understanding of employees' perceptions and the beginning of a dialogue about how officer perks could be curtailed during the lean times. For example, guidelines were developed for appropriate use of the helicopter. And the executive vice president who had hosted the meeting began to ask for Watkins' input more often. "He knew that if he asked me something that I would be very straightforward and honest," she said.

This reputation has paid off for Watkins. "I'm considered the person you go to if you want honest answers," she said. "I don't know how not to be honest, so yes, I will tell people what I think. It's not about slander—it's about candor. I do it in a thoughtful and careful way."

Watkins' commitment to honesty was evident earlier in her career as well. While working as an assistant to a regional manager at another company, she took a vacation day in the middle of the week in order to celebrate her mother's 80th birthday. When she returned to work the next day, Watkins' boss called her into his office and was "livid" that she had not responded to his pages to her while she was out for the day. He explained that the company was on a "24/7 operation," and he expected her to be accessible even on her vacation days.

With little hesitation, Watkins closed the door to her boss's office and told him that she had worked hard enough to earn her vacation and that she wasn't taking advantage of anything. It was her day and she chose to devote it to her mother, Watkins said. She went on to explain her value system, namely that family came first.

"I even said to him, 'If this is a problem, it's good for us to work it out now, because it's not going to change.' I told him I was willing to leave that position and go someplace else in the company."

Even at the time, Watkins was aware that she risked losing her job or at least creating a barrier between her boss and herself. Instead, she worked another four years for him, and their relationship benefited from the initial honest exchange. "Our conversations changed, because he realized I'd always tell him the truth," she recalls. "From then on, we had a very honest and authentic relationship. And he even stopped taking his pager when he went on vacation!"

In her current leadership role, Watkins—named by The Atlanta Business League as one of Atlanta's "100 Most Influential Women" for the past 4 years—continues to always tell the truth, but she's also learned to consider her audience, carefully discerning how much honest information her followers can handle.

Leaders who are committed to establishing trust and credibility through transparency have to make complicated decisions about just how transparent to be, and finding the optimal level that respects both the good of the individual and that of the whole organization is difficult to do. Yet there is no gray area in the value of honesty—a leader must never stray from the truth, even if it means saying, "I know, but I can't tell you right now."

Of all the expectations people have of credible leaders, honesty is the most critical. Even a single misstep in honesty can be very difficult and perhaps impossible to overcome, depending on how serious the infraction is. And no matter how perfectly you meet the other eight expectations of credibility, you will never be perceived as credible if you are caught telling lies.

## THE TRUTH ABOUT HONESTY

Think you're honest? We all do. I rarely meet anyone who doesn't believe that he or she is a good, old-fashioned, truth-telling citizen. However, if you are a truly honest person, then you are a rarity, because studies on dishonest behavior assert that practically everyone is something of a fibber if not an out-and-out liar. Consider

❏ In a survey of 40,000 people, 93 percent admitted to lying "regularly and habitually" in the workplace (*Fast Company*, 9/97).

❏ College students admit that at least 70 percent of their excuses for missed assignments are lies (*Psychology Today*, 11/2002).

❑ Of 12,750 workers, only 63 percent feel that their companies conduct business with honesty and integrity (*BusinessWeek*, 9/2/2002).

To be credible, you must be *overwhelmingly honest*—so honest that people never question whether what you say is the truth as you know it. And if this weren't difficult enough, you must be overwhelmingly honest in ways that show respect and care for people. Doing all this—especially in today's complicated world—requires tremendous skill, practice, and fortitude.

In their landmark book on credibility, authors and leadership experts James Kouzes and Barry Posner wrote: "Of all the attributes of credibility, however, there is one that is unquestionably of greatest importance. The dimension of honesty accounts for more of the variance in believability than all of the other factors combined" (*Credibility*, Jossey-Bass, San Francisco, 1993, p. 24).

You may be a person who "wants the best" for all, who is sincerely kind, and who seeks understanding and keeps promises, but if you veer from the truth—even for the "good" reasons of not wanting to hurt another's feelings or wanting things to go smoothly—your credibility will suffer.

Matthew, a charismatic 56-year-old who has held leadership positions in several industries for more than 30 years, knows how crucial honesty is to his performance as a leader. "I had an experience very early in my career that changed me and made me become totally committed to honesty," he once confided. As a young division manager at a consumer products company, Matthew had selected Jim, who seemed capable and well liked, as his new sales manager, but within a few months, Matthew realized that he had misjudged Jim's abilities for a managerial position. Still, Matthew supported Jim and tried to manage the sales team through him. A year later Jim sat across from Matthew and angrily described a year of struggle and disappointment. "You knew from the start that I was not qualified to do this job, and you sat by and said nothing. You should have told me," Jim told Matthew. Rather than tell Jim the truth early on, Matthew had chosen to "let the situation play out."

Despite Matthew's best intentions, his lack of honesty resulted in the loss of an employee whose other talents Matthew valued and could have benefited the company in other ways. Matthew's company had to invest in replacing Jim, and the team had to suffer through the transition. It was a hard lesson for Matthew, but it stuck. "When I'm faced with the difficult choice of telling the truth or avoiding it, I always see Jim's face in front of me. Then the choice seems easy—I tell the truth."

A leader's ability to build a history of consistently telling the truth correlates directly with the level of trust others have for that leader. And trust is vital to motivating and influencing others, making leaders' truth-telling skills indicative not only of their personal reputation but also of their entire organization's level of success.

And yet, individuals often miss the mark in assessing how honest others believe them to be. We believe that we are honest just like we believe that we are nice. To think otherwise would challenge our whole sense of self. How do you rate your ability to be honest in all transactions? How would others rate you?

## HOW HONEST ARE YOU, REALLY?

Using the following scale, rate each expectation of credible leaders in two ways:

How well do you think you are doing at meeting the expectation?

What might others think about how well you are meeting the expectation?

**SCALE:** 1 = significant improvement needed; 2 = slight improvement needed; 3 = skilled/competent; 4 = talented; 5 = outstanding: a role model

| EXPECTATION | HOW DO YOU THINK YOU ARE DOING? | WHAT MIGHT OTHERS THINK? |
|---|---|---|
| Communicates in a direct and straightforward manner. | 1 2 3 4 5 | 1 2 3 4 5 |
| Demonstrates honest and ethical behavior in all transactions. | 1 2 3 4 5 | 1 2 3 4 5 |
| Promotes truth telling within the organization through behaviors and expectations. | 1 2 3 4 5 | 1 2 3 4 5 |
| Tells the whole truth despite the consequences (i.e., avoids white lies). | 1 2 3 4 5 | 1 2 3 4 5 |
| Does not exaggerate, "spin," or stretch the truth. | 1 2 3 4 5 | 1 2 3 4 5 |
| Tells the truth while maintaining tactfulness. | 1 2 3 4 5 | 1 2 3 4 5 |

**MY SCORES:**

*Scoring yourself:* Add your total for each column. A single column score of 27 to 30 suggests that you are doing an exceptional job and meeting others' expectations of someone who is overwhelmingly honest. A column score of 22 to 26 indicates that you have some areas for improvement; on issues important as these, I believe leaders should strive to be "outstanding: a role model." Below 22 indicates a danger area, and you may be chipping away at your credibility. A discrepancy of more than 7 points between the two column totals indicates a possible gap in perception worth investigating. If your "How do you think you are doing?" score is higher than your "What might others think?" score, your intentions may be better than your actions. If your "What might others think?" score is higher, you may not be giving yourself enough credit for a job well done.

How others perceive our level of honesty is ultimately hard to gauge without their actual input. The truth about how others perceive you may surprise you. In leadership assessments, over 50 percent of 13,000 peers and direct reports felt that their leaders could improve in being honest and ethical.

**In leadership assessments, over 50 percent of 13,000 peers and direct reports felt that their leaders could improve in being honest and ethical.**

When leaders learn that others do not perceive them to be as honest as they themselves believe they are, defenses kick in. Tony, a vice president in a large health care organization, did not like seeing the breakout of his 360-assessment scores on honesty. In our coaching session, he fussed and fumed. Why didn't others agree with his rating? Why, after working with him for more than 5 years, did some of his direct reports and colleagues sit on the fence, "neither satisfied nor dissatisfied" with this behavior? Who *was* that person who marked "highly dissatisfied" on the item inquiring about Tony's level of honesty? "And there's my damn boss," he said pointing to the graph indicating his manager's rating of 4. "I thought we had a good relationship. How come he didn't give me a 5?"

Even getting the truth about honesty, it seems, is not always easy, especially when we are assessing our own truth-telling behaviors. We misjudge our own level of honesty for two reasons: We have an inherent desire to believe that we are good, and dishonesty is so rampant that our tolerance for it in ourselves as well as others (particularly when it is in the form of casual white lies) is fairly high.

## LEADERSHIP DILEMMAS

There's nothing casual or white about a lie that leads to stock devaluation, job loss, or a company's demise. The allure of money, success, and power cause many a good leader to blow it. But what about business situations that present problems not so black and white as whether or not to participate in insider trading or accounting fraud? Leaders and nonleaders often face dilemmas that are not only right versus wrong but also ones that seem to be right versus right. The toughest choices are those that pit one "right" against another.

Consider the following situations:

❑ An employee is asked by her manager to explain why her team's project is late, but a truthful explanation would reveal personal information that was given in confidence by one of her team members. Should she be truthful, or should she honor her commitment to confidentiality?

❑ A manager must decide whether to fire an employee who lied about his past work experience—the disciplinary action required by the company's handbook—or whether to overlook the incident after learning about the employee's desperate need for the job and its health care benefits to provide for his sick daughter.

Sometimes being dishonest seems like the better choice. But keep in mind: Honesty is a universal ethic, accepted by all cultures and religions as the *right* choice. In his book, *How Good People Make Tough Choices*, ethicist Rushworth M. Kidder explains that a departure from the truth is always a right-versus-wrong dilemma, with lying always being a wrong.

When leaders are not supported by an organization with a core value of honesty that is explicit and lived, choosing to be honest can be even more difficult. As a middle manager in a large manufacturing plant, Eileen is aware that salary cuts in her department are imminent. However, her boss has told her "not to breathe a word." In fact, she was told that if asked, she should tell her people "it's not going to happen," and she has been warned about repercussions if she does not do as she has been told. Eileen's situation pits her reputation against her future with the company. Her credibility will suffer when people find out that she has been lying to them. What does she do? Unfortunately, she must choose between being honest, maintaining her integrity and credibility, and bucking her boss and possibly losing her job.

People often lie at work because they are afraid of retribution. They think that to speak the truth or "tell it like it is" is career suicide. Or they believe that honesty will not do any good because nothing will change anyway—and actually, sometimes they are right. In October 2002, an Aquila, Inc., employee was fired 2 hours after he responded to the CEO's organization-wide e-mail encouraging workers to send their "thoughts and concerns" about the utility company. In a response e-mail, the employee, Stephen Millan, questioned whether a $7.6 million severance package for a recently departed CEO (who was the new CEO's brother) was ethical at a time when Aquila was making various cutbacks to save money, including removing free hot chocolate from company break rooms. Perhaps Millan overstepped an ethical line himself when he also copied several of his coworkers on the e-mail to the CEO. Aquila's message was clear, however: Speak the truth, and be prepared for harsh consequences (*Kansas City Star*, 10/5/2002). Is honesty always rewarded? No, not always. The truth can set you free, but it also can challenge the status quo, make people angry, and even get you fired.

Leaders with credibility are expected to always be honest, no matter the consequences, because it is the right thing to do—not because it will get them something. And yet

❏ In recent assessment surveys, only 26 percent of more than 4800 employees were highly satisfied with their leader's performance in communicating in a direct and straightforward manner.

❏ According to a survey of over 2000 U.S. workers, less than half believe that their senior leaders are people of high integrity (Hudson Institute).

❏ A survey of 12,750 employees from all job levels and major industries found that less than half of employees think senior management is honest (Watson Wyatt, February 2002).

If CEO salaries were based on perceptions of honesty rather than meeting revenue targets and improving shareholder value, it appears that most would be shopping at St. Vincent's Thrift Shops.

Leaders are often privy to information that others are not. When they are in situations in which their direct reports or colleagues prod for information that cannot be revealed, many play the fool: "I don't know."

"Sometimes I feel I'm not getting all the information available," one executive said of her boss. "I begin to get the sense that she's working another agenda than the one being discussed. Then I start feeling that if I've told her something confidential, it might not remain confidential. The lack of trust begins to bleed over into everything."

In recent assessment surveys, only 26 percent of more than 4800 employees were highly satisfied with their leader's performance in communicating in a direct and straightforward manner.

When leaders are evasive, relationships suffer. And yet there are other options. To increase or maintain credibility, a leader must be honest in all transactions; however, honesty does *not* demand full disclosure. When a leader knows something and is unable to be fully transparent, the honest answer is "I know, but I can't tell you." A leader's commitment to honesty while still maintaining the required confidentiality will be respected and appreciated.

When faced with a messy situation that you are not prepared for, consider the vastly underused option of saying "No. I can't discuss this right now" or "I'm unable to reveal that information" or "I'm committed to being honest with you, but I need some time to think about this before responding." If appropriate, help your listeners to understand why you cannot discuss the topic.

Also understand that a commitment to honesty requires leaders to give followers opportunities to ask for it. Following a reorganization at a major beverage company, Pat, a senior executive, held a meeting with her division. Morale was low, and there were rumors of more layoffs to come. Because Pat did not want to be confronted with questions she could not answer, she did not allow a question-and-answer session to take place. Consequently, her credibility took a hit—she was perceived as withholding information and not caring about people who were rightfully concerned and even confused. A better choice would have been to allow questions and to answer them honestly—even if the answer had been "I can't give that information at this time."

## BUILDING AN HONEST CULTURE

Half of the 12 people around the conference table sat there more than a little stunned. It was a meeting of key decision makers from a division of an Atlanta-based manufacturer, a 220-person unit with more than $1.5 billion in sales, and one of its biggest customers, a Fortune 50 company. The customer's buyers and vice president, long accustomed to the manufacturer bending over backwards to please them, were listening to Tricia, the Atlanta company's lead representative, surprisingly, albeit respectfully, explaining that the two companies would have to change the way they did business. "We had been working very hard to grow our sales with them, but we didn't feel the progress," Tricia said. "They were consuming a lot of our products, but frankly, they weren't a very profitable customer. In the past, we had rarely challenged any of their requests, even when they ate away at profitability and drove a higher cost to service them."

Prior to the meeting, Tricia and her team had determined that their customer must commit to being more stable and predictable—offering better forecasting, for example—in order for the relationship to continue. They also needed a "broader bundle of products, products that had more margin and more value to offset the high volume commodity purchases." It was a difficult conversation and a risky demand for Tricia to make. After all, the client could have reacted indignantly and ceased doing business with her company.

Instead, the customer's vice president took Tricia's words very seriously, supported her needs, gave direction to his people to outline specific needs, and began working with Tricia's team to change the business model. "It didn't happen overnight, but things changed," Tricia said. "Before that meeting, we did everything they asked for without really understanding the economic impact. But afterwards, we had a more honest relationship with them as opposed to just doing everything they wanted."

The honest exchange, Tricia believed, also had a positive impact on her team. "It showed them that having those kinds of difficult conversations was important to improving business and that if we are prepared and honest with the facts, we can help our customers help us."

Italian politician Antonio Gramsci once said, "Telling the truth is always revolutionary." Credible leaders not only tell the truth; they also promote honesty throughout the organization. They are zealous hunting dogs of truth, sniffing out misunderstandings before they happen, digging for dishonesty, and constantly looking for secrets. People who are honest enough to be called *credible* lead the way and make things better for others by making honesty safe. They know that an honest culture breeds a trusting workplace. And when people trust each other in the workplace, business thrives.

A leader cannot assume that honest and straightforward communication exists naturally in an organization. I work with teams to create guiding principles—written statements that describe what must be present to work together successfully. Guiding principles always contain one or more vows to tell the truth. Team members commit to be "honest" and "direct and straightforward," to "keep no secrets," and to "not shoot the messenger." Some ask, "Why do we have to do this? Don't we all just know this anyway?" Perhaps, but credible leaders know that this assumption can be a dangerous communication sinkhole. Creating an honest culture requires formal commitments and diligent, deliberate effort day after day.

In his final remarks to his sales team at an annual sales meeting, Wes, a vice president at a major insurer, got everyone's attention when he said: "And oh, by the way. Lie to me . . . and you're gonna die." He repeated the last three words for emphasis while everyone sat a little more upright in their chairs. "I mean it," he went on. "Lie to me, and it's over." Anyone who works for Wes knows how important the truth is. If you do not choose honesty, you may still be breathing, but you will not have a job working with Wes.

Not every push for honesty has to be as stern and serious as Wes's. There are other effective strategies that make people feel safe telling the truth.

## Pay for It

Deanna Berg, Ph.D., an expert in group dynamics and innovation, gives pennies to senior leaders to emphasize visually how important it is for everyone on the team to be open and honest and "put in their two cents." Her idea encourages people to say what they are thinking and has inspired many leaders to put a pile of pennies in the middle of the conference table in their team meetings. "The effect can be most interesting," a senior executive who tried this technique relates. Reaching toward the middle of the table to the pile of coins, one of his team members slowly counted out 10 pennies as the rest of the group stared. "What I am going to say," he said, "is a lot more than two cents worth." And it was. Later, a coworker acknowledged his courage and said, "Thanks for saying what we were all thinking but afraid to say."

## Ask Leading Questions

Rarely is everything put on the table, so the truth must be sought constantly. Try to encourage and engage your followers in honest discussions by asking leading questions. For example, one executive always ends his meetings with, "What's left under the table?" One leader opens meetings by asking, "What do I need to know that I might not want to hear?" Rather than stopping there, he continues to dig: "Is there more? What else? Is there another piece?" Consider making a habit of asking such questions. Do it in a way that feels comfortable to you. Sometimes people will respond; sometimes they won't. People are not always going to say everything that is on their minds, but that's not the point. Credible leaders elevate honesty as a vital, trust-building value; they model it, and they help others to do the same.

## Model Vulnerability

Peter Porcelli, senior vice president of income development at the Eastern Division of the American Cancer Society in New Jersey, learned from a 360-degree assessment that his eight team members wanted him to do a better job in developing their talent. However, he wasn't sure what that meant exactly or how to go about making an improvement. He tried asking each of his three direct reports for their answers, gave them some time to think of their response, and then followed up with a second conversation. "I find this very stressful," one of his direct reports said. "I think the world of you as my boss, and it's hard for me to tell you how to be better." But she did. Peter discovered that she wanted more exposure to senior-level executives and more support on a new initiative on which she had worked. By seeking out the truth, Peter received tangible suggestions on how to improve as a leader and had a valuable, honest exchange with a follower, who likely felt an increased respect for Peter.

## Take the Hot Seat

Sometimes a leader can benefit from a more intense exchange of honesty, and I will suggest that they take the "hot seat" in front of all their team members, who have spent up to 3 hours with me developing a list of suggestions for performance improvement. It takes courage, but some leaders are willing to take the plunge. Jason, a telecommunications executive, was one such leader.

Let's examine the case of Jason, a manager I recently coached. In a conference room, Jason introduced me to all 12 of his direct reports as a facilitator who would lead them in a discussion. He told them that he needed help being a better leader and posed three questions, based on information he received in a 360-degree assessment:

1. How can I better develop the talent on this team?

2. I think I am good at listening to bad news, but my feedback suggests otherwise. Help me to understand this.

3. How can I be a better leader to this team?

After Jason left the room, I got out my markers, walked to the flip chart, and said: "In the spirit of friendship and honesty, let's get some answers for Jason." Although they were hesitant at first, Jason's team quickly embraced the opportunity, and the truth unfolded. Flip-chart pages covered walls, and soon it was time to summarize the information.

As I always do in these situations, I gave the team options for how to communicate their summary of information to Jason. They can choose a team member to be their spokesperson, or they can elect me to do it. As is usually the case, Jason's team chose me to disseminate the feedback. Next, I did a sort of dress rehearsal, which allowed team members to change the order of their messages, give me examples, rewrite the flip-chart pages that would be given to Jason, and massage the script. "Use 'difficult' because 'pigheaded' sounds too harsh," one member said.

The honest dialogue that generally ensues between the leader on the hot seat and his or her team can be extremely powerful. An IBM executive who once went through what Jason went through said to me: "I've jumped off telephone poles with my team. I've done all of Covey's stuff and spent a month at Harvard to learn how to be a better leader. But this experience was the most powerful." Indeed, this method of getting to the truth can benefit the entire group, not just the leader. Long after the hot-seat event, people often say things like, "We're able to speak more honestly with one another."

Ginger Graham, former president and CEO of medical device manufacturer Advanced Cardiovascular Systems, which spun out from Eli Lilly in 1994 as Guidant Corporation, described in a recent *Harvard Business Review* article a similar process in her organization. Each member of the senior management team would take turns sitting on a tall stool in front of the room, and while on the stool, they were only allowed to listen. In turn, peers bring up a shortcoming they observed and offer suggestions for improvement. Graham believed it to be one of the most powerful tools for building mutual accountability and honest communication. "Speaking the truth is the highest form of respect for an individual," she wrote. She also saw a benefit for the larger organization. "As a result of this public exercise in truth telling, those of us who took the feedback to heart dramatically improved our leadership skill," she wrote. "And the performance of the entire organization improved" ("If You Want Honesty, Break Some Rules,"*Harvard Business Review,* April 2002).

## Be Diligent About Keeping Followers Informed

When employees are enlightened—for example, they understand the state of the industry and what's required to keep their company afloat—then even downsizing does not seem like such a random and cruel act. Being more forthcoming about company information also slows the rumor mill. When people are left in the dark, they generally fill the black holes with their own—mostly negative—interpretations.

Truth telling in organizations can be difficult, and leaders often have to wrestle with complicated issues before being forthcoming. And yet honesty—or its resulting flow of reliable information—is no longer just admired ethical behavior but is fast becoming imperative to business success. While a lack of honesty does not always lead to outright fraud or a damaging scandal, it can lead to ineffective meetings, cynicism, low morale, and missed opportunities. When trying to create a safe place for honesty, leaders who model honesty bring top results.

## SPEAKING HONESTLY AS A LEADER

Can a person be "too honest"? This is a tricky question. Usually the phrase *too honest* is a criticism of a person's delivery rather than of the actual content of a truthful message. Be careful not to fall too far toward "honesty for honesty's sake." An extreme example of this would be telling a colleague that his or her presentation was weak because "Well, it was, and I thought she should know." Before offering "painful truth," especially when it is unsolicited, ask yourself: Am I giving this person valuable information that will benefit him or her? Is this the right time and place to communicate this information? The truth must be extended in a caring and sensitive way. You must tell the truth responsibly. Honesty without tact can put a dull stain on your good intentions. Being honest is a virtue that pays dividends in trust for companies and individuals, but the truth must be told with care.

A leader's followers are usually very cognizant of how well he or she tells the truth:

❏ Janette is a successful regional vice president at a telecommunications provider who gets high marks for being honest but low marks in how she does it. "Janette is not a malicious person," said one of her employees. "She just regularly demonstrates thoughtlessness."

❏ People who work for Tom praised their boss for being honest, communicating directly, and holding people accountable. But he could be a bit more tactful, they said. "He's a very good leader with a good personality, but in certain situations he is a bit too direct and needs to handle the situation in a more caring way."

❏ Giselle, on the other hand, has an approach to honesty that is highly regarded. Her five direct reports sing her praises: "She brings a certain grace to every situation. Without whitewashing the situation, she delivers the truth with an abundance of tact."

What might your direct reports or peers say about how you deliver the truth? If you are described as "too honest" or "too direct," ask someone you trust about what behaviors accompany your delivery of the truth. This is likely where your problem lies.

Two other leaders have just the opposite problem, yet it is one that is probably equally disrespectful:

❏ Tony is an engineer in charge of laying cable for a telecommunications company. In this competitive industry, Tony faces lots of deadlines and resulting stress. I was hired as a coach to help him communicate "more clearly and concisely" for his monthly presentations to his 16 colleagues. However, I discovered that Tony had a bigger problem. At the end of his presentations, he often was asked questions that made him uncomfortable. And his replies reflected his discomfort: "Well, the answer is yes and no. It's actually a little of this and a little of that." Because Tony's answers were not concrete, people felt that he was being evasive. Tony's "nonanswers" were eroding his credibility. In his 360-degree report, an employee wrote: "He should be forthcoming with information about the actual situation. If he does, that will build trust. If he doesn't do that, we think he is hiding the truth."

❏ Ken, a vice president at an advertising agency, had good intentions with his employees, but he failed in being honest enough. He was criticized by his direct reports for being "too careful" with his words, even too "politically correct." We should all choose our words carefully, but Ken took it too far and consequently came across as being evasive and "too indirect." In coaching Ken, I had to teach him that he could not convince people of his honesty while tiptoeing. Ken had to get comfortable with telling the truth not only to meet the expectations of credibility but also to help cultivate an environment where others feel safe in being honest.

Being honest in a caring and direct way, especially when it is a very difficult thing to do, demonstrates to people that you think enough of them to tell the truth and are not willing to compromise the integrity of the relationship.

## DAILY DISTORTIONS

Deception comes in different shapes and sizes, from outright lies and exaggerations to evasions and half-truths. Some dishonesty comes in the form of casual informalities, lies so common that we actually have come to *expect* them. Julia Kirby, editor of *Harvard Business Review*, feels that there has been a "disturbing tolerance of—and even collusion with—some forms of dishonesty" (*ComputerWorld*, 3/11/2002). She warns of a tolerance shift: "We're not going from black to white, but there's a really important shift in the gray area."

You might ask, "But aren't white lies all right?" Whether it's gray areas or white lies, we seem to be justifying our lies with color coding. When social niceties bleed over into dishonesty, people can become suspicious. How many times have you heard, "I was just going to call you!" and wondered, *Really?*

Dishonesty is useful for making lives easier. "Oh you have that new software? I want to load it on my computer, too." Let's face it, we are immune to those scary warning labels. Consider our excuses: "I don't think I received that e-mail." "My secretary must have forgotten to put it on the calendar." "I thought it was okay to share that." Telling someone that you can't do lunch with them because you have a meeting may be more comfortable than telling them the real reason—that you are having lunch with a mutual friend and do not want to feel obliged to make it a threesome. And excusing tardiness to a meeting with "terrible traffic" is easier than suffering your boss's disapproval of the real reason—you overslept. Let's face it, we are so blasé about our lies that we do not even try to be original.

While daily distortions may not be on the scale of an Enron lie, they still chip away at credibility. If earning credibility is your priority, you must break current codes of conduct and climb to the high road of honesty. Here are some tips for getting there:

❑ *Take note.* So many of our daily distortions are just lazy habits. Start paying close attention to what you say. Ask yourself at regular intervals in your day: Have I said anything that is not exactly true? If you did, examine why you said it, and consider what you could have said instead.

❑ *Think first.* Ending daily distortions takes commitment and discipline. Try to remain mindful while you interact with others.

❑ *Pledge accountability.* Commit to being honest even when doing so might make you appear less than perfect.

❑ *Swap kind truths for fake praises.* Some people compliment carelessly. Be thoughtful and sincere with your kindness. Maybe "You've got really strong speaking skills, and I liked the way you opened your presentation" is more truthful than "That was the best customer pitch I've ever seen!" A desire to make others feel good about themselves is an admirable quality, and others will appreciate your praises most when they perceive you to be sincere.

A person who chooses honesty in the "little" ways not only will appear more truthful than others on a daily basis, but he or she will be better prepared to remain honest even when the stakes get high.

## HONESTY AS YOUR CORE VALUE

Whether you are managing people, negotiating a contract, or selling a product, doing business presents situations in which evading the truth, exaggerating, diluting, spinning, or flat-out lying seem appropriate, acceptable, and logical.

❑ Dennis loves his job selling medical equipment, and he is good at it. "When the doctor asks me if that's the best price, I say yes, but that's not really true," he admits. "The price could always be lower." Is Dennis a great salesman or a liar? The answer: Both.

❑ Sharon, a colleague, tells me about a project she was being considered for. "I told them my fee was X, but that's not true. I'll do it for much less. We'll see what happens!" In a situation in which the truth really is not expected anyway, is lying still lying? The answer: Yes.

You have a choice, of course. You can practice certain measures of deception and possibly never get caught. People may not even care that you bend the truth. They may see it as "part of doing business." A national survey of 2390 workers found that 38 percent believed that their managers would authorize illegal or unethical conduct to meet business goals (Fast Company, September 2000).

Being honest can be burdensome. The fact remains, however, that it is an essential component of credibility.

Our nation's recent bubble-bursting corporate and political scandals have replaced many rose-colored glasses with high-powered magnifiers. As prevalent as untruths have come to be, the sting that a lie leaves has not lost its potency. *No one* wants to be lied to. When we are, we rarely forget.

If you are unable to be fully transparent, you can still adhere to principles of honesty by offering as much information as you can, including why full transparency is not possible. Do not leave your followers to wonder about possible hidden agendas.

While truth telling in organizations can be complicated and messy, honesty must be an unbroken guiding principle, the hub on the leadership wheel. And it must be visibly demonstrated through actions and decisions, or trust and credibility will not exist.

# CHAPTER 3

# Gather Intelligence

*You did the best that you knew how.*
*Now that you know better, you'll do better.*

—Maya Angelou

Mike Silvers had no idea his loud voice made employees cringe in discomfort. After growing up the oldest of six brothers and working in a steel factory for a while, speaking loudly became a sort of code in his DNA. At 48-years-old, however, as the head of the largest branch of the Vista Federal Credit Union, which serves all of Disney's 60,000 "cast members," Silver's loud voice made his employees think he was yelling at them, and this seemingly inconsistent miscommunication was causing some subtle discomfort among his team members and was affecting his leadership effectiveness. Silvers came to realize this through a formal feedback process in which he asked his team how he could improve as their leader. Now Silvers and his team are so comfortable with asking for and giving feedback that his staff simply will give him a downward motion with their hands if his voice level gets too loud.

Through anonymous 360-degree performance surveys, Silvers realized a lot more about how his staff perceived him as a leader, and he learned that by changing what were genuinely unintentional bad habits, he could vastly improve his relationships and effectiveness. For example, when the lobby is packed with customers—Disney employees—and Silvers sees one of his service representatives working at her desk without a customer sitting with her, Silvers used to walk briskly to her desk and ask, "Are you ready to take another member?" Through his leadership coach, Karen Walker, a consultant with Atlanta-based Assessment Plus, Inc., who has a Ph.D. in psychology, Silvers learned that his staff felt he was micromanaging and that he did not trust them to do a good job.

"I talked with them, and we all came to an agreement," he said. "I told them, 'Okay, I'm going to trust that when a customer is in the lobby, and he or she is not sitting with you at your desk, it's because you're quickly finishing up paperwork from the last customer before inviting him or her over.'"

Silvers explained how letting go and giving them the decision-making power was difficult for him, and Dr. Walker concurred: "He's a real driver, and he's very enthusiastic about his work." However, Silvers managed to make the change, and in doing so, he saw an almost immediate decrease in the time between customers being serviced. "I showed by my actions that I trusted them, and production went up."

Asking for feedback, informally and formally (through surveys), became status quo for Silvers, and consequently, he believes that his relationships with his staff, his peers, and even his boss have improved. Increased scores in a subsequent assessment survey certainly seemed to confirm his progress.

When we discover how others perceive us, we are better able to align our intentions with reality and develop a plan for improvement. In order to learn and grow, we must have self-awareness, which, ironically, requires input from others. "The paradox of self-awareness is that one cannot become self-aware through self alone," wrote Deepak Sethi, director of executive and leadership development for the Thomson Corp., a $6-billion, 40,000-employee information publishing company (*Learning Journeys*, Palo Alto, CA, 2000, Davies-Black Publishing, p. 85).

Asking others for their opinions about something conveys respect. When the subject is you, you practice a key aspect of transparency and show others that you value them, increasing your respect and credibility.

## WE'RE NOT ASKING

In leadership surveys of 559 managers, 86 percent of 6023 of their followers and peers said that those leaders could improve at regularly asking for feedback.

Executive coach Tom Heinselman recalled for me a time when he was "out of bullets" during a coaching session with an executive, Phil, who had been extremely successful in opening new cellular markets and executing turnarounds in failing markets. This leader, according to the data from his performance assessments, also was a lousy listener, thought he had all the good ideas, and was obnoxious and abusive to people.

> **In leadership surveys of 559 managers, 86 percent of 6023 of their followers and peers said that those leaders could improve at regularly asking for feedback.**

"Look, why do I care about this?" Phil asked Tom. "I'm the most successful startup manager in the company. When it counts, they call me. If this is how these people feel, why am I so successful leading them through these tough assignments?"

Tom pointed out that people clamor to get behind Phil because he is their ticket, but they will move on or celebrate his demise because he is not inspiring loyalty.

Phil was unmoved by this logic, and Tom struggled for a way to make this executive see the value in his feedback.

"When you die, do you want people to attend your funeral for business reasons only?" It was a question Marshall Goldsmith, Tom's colleague, used with success on a $6-million-per-year Wall Street Gordon Gekko type who was so shaken by it that he had made a dramatic turnaround.

This time Phil hesitated before responding. "Funny you should say that," he said. "A few weeks back, I drove up to a funeral where people were spilling out of the church, and I told myself that I wouldn't have this problem when I died."

Tom had another client, the head of executive development at a Fortune 100 firm, who would not agree to undergo formal feedback, even though all his staff and managers were doing it, and Tom suggested that he should, too, if only to set the right leadership example. The client replied: "Tom, you obviously don't understand my role here. You see, I don't *get* feedback. I *give* feedback."

These "I'm better than you" messages can worm their way through an organization, devaluing the feedback process and destroying a culture's values that promote learning, professional growth, and transparency.

Other leaders fail to ask for feedback not because of hubris but because they simply do not see the point. "I don't ask because I'm sure that if there was something I needed to know, they'd tell me," the managing partner of an insurance firm once told me. Yet that same leader's followers confirmed that they would only do such a thing if they "didn't care about having a job the next day."

Other leaders have insisted that they ask for feedback all the time, and again, their direct reports would give a contradictory message. Obviously, there is a disconnect if leaders say that they ask, and the people they work with are not hearing the invitation. Ultimately, however, most leaders do not ask for input for two reasons: They are not sure that they want the answers, or they do not feel comfortable asking in the first place.

Why don't leaders want the answers that might reveal valuable information that is critical for future success? Their reasoning often stems from seven myths of feedback.

## Myth 1: If They're Right, Then I'm Wrong

Perceptions may differ from person to person and may be opposite from how you see yourself. Feedback is not necessarily right or wrong. Remember that others are judging you against their own experience, context, and values.

## Myth 2: My Personality Will Have to Change

Feedback is rarely offered in an attempt to fundamentally change someone's makeup. Most people think that this is impossible anyway. Usually people give feedback hoping that you will fine-tune certain aspects of your personality—not change it altogether. For example, someone might ask you to speak up more in meetings, but they likely will not request that you turn your quiet self into a member of the Osborne family.

## Myth 3: They'll Point Out All My Mistakes

Feedback is not a detailed analysis of your past or present mistakes. If you have made some—and all of us do—they likely came with some negative fallout. Formal feedback surveys actually can help you to gauge the extent and intensity of what people might be feeling as a result of your misstep. How upset is your team about your failure to deal with a particular under-performer? You might be relieved to find that the issue is barely a blip on their radar screens. Or you might learn that an incident is still stewing and that more patchup is necessary.

## Myth 4: I'll Have to Do Something I Don't Want to Do

While asking for input requires confidence, humility, and a respect for others' opinions, it does not require you to respond with action steps that you feel are undesirable, uncomfortable, or impossible. I will talk more about this later in this chapter.

## Myth 5: I Already Know What They'll Say

There is almost always a discrepancy between the self we think we are and the self that is perceived by the rest of the world. In receiving feedback, you likely will get a picture of yourself that will be more accurate than the one you have now. And others' comments not only may surprise you, but they also may validate your worth far better than you do.

## Myth 6: They'll Take It as an Opportunity to Get Back at Me

In my experience coaching almost 3000 men and women, feedback that is spiteful and revengeful is as rare as having a fish jump in my kayak. (It happened once.) People generally offer a fair assessment of the behaviors they are asked to rate and thoughtful replies to questions posed. They often also express a warm regard for the person being assessed.

### Myth 7: This Is Going to Hurt

Actually, it might, but only in the short term. While you likely will not be squashed by a litany of your deficits and faults, you could be disappointed or angry about what you are told. Asking for feedback takes courage, and anyone who thinks otherwise is kidding themselves. In expansive, expensive corner offices, as well as in windowless cubicles, I have seen jaws quiver, knees jerk, eyes brim with tears, and more than a little defensiveness surface as I have reviewed feedback reports with leaders. In the long run, however, you will be far better off knowing how you are perceived by people who are playing often critical roles in your future success.

# THE PAYBACKS

Take the story of the high school principal who had sterling feedback from his direct reports. This man had more than 50 people reporting to him—teachers, custodians, and cafeteria workers—and all thought that he was terrific and told him so in anonymous surveys.

"How in the world have you managed to create an environment where people look to you as their leader and give you such a big thumb's up?" the principal was asked.

"I've learned that even the PTA has a good idea every now and then. So I always ask."

Consider the following situations:

❑ At the end of a weekly operational meeting, your chief executive officer (CEO) stands and says that he would like to take a moment to thank each of you for the feedback he received on his leadership surveys. "I learned a lot about myself. It was not easy. In fact, it was hard. But it's important for me to be the best leader I can be for this company and for you. I appreciate your honesty."

❑ Your spouse sits you down on the back deck on a summer day and notes that you have an upcoming anniversary. "There's nothing more important to me than our relationship, and I want it to continue to grow and be the best it can be. I'm asking for some guidance. I want to know what you think I do well as your partner and what things I could do better. Will you give it some thought?"

❑ A successful colleague you admire has an important budget presentation to the executive committee next week. "I value your opinion," he says to you. "Would you come to a rehearsal I've set up on Wednesday? I'd like your help on how I can make it better."

Wouldn't we all feel extremely good if these situations happened in our lives? We would feel valued and important.

There is power in behaviors that say, "I want your opinion. You count." This message taps into a fundamental need people have to feel as if they matter. When you ask others for personal or professional feedback, you also send another underlying message: "I don't know it all. I'm not perfect. Help me see what I might not know. Help me be more successful." You demonstrate humility, a willingness to be open and transparent, and a desire to serve and to learn.

And it is the learning that is perhaps the biggest payoff of asking others for feedback. In surveys, 95 percent of leaders were unable to give themselves the highest rating on having a firm understanding of their own strengths and weaknesses, and 98 percent of their bosses agreed. Asking others about their strengths and weaknesses helps leaders gain a

> In surveys, 95 percent of leaders were unable to give themselves the highest rating on having a firm understanding of their own strengths and weaknesses, and 98 percent of their bosses agreed.

more solid understanding of what they are doing well and what might need to be improved.

By asking for feedback, leaders experience the following benefits.

## Seeing What Others See

As a young sales manager, Emily was shocked and dismayed to learn through formal feedback that one of her seven sales reps believed that she could be dishonest and unethical in her business practices. After some strategic thinking, she pursued one-on-one conversations with two reps, Jim and Roger, with whom she had close relationships. "What have I done or what am I doing that is being perceived as dishonest and unethical?" Both men told the same story.

When reps would deliver an order late in the month after unit and personal quotas were met, Emily often would say, "Why don't you just hold this order until next week, and we'll get a fast start next month." Although Jim and Roger were fine with this, another rep, who they did not name, thought it was dishonest. He believed that you should book the business when you got it. And he wondered what else was being done behind closed doors that might be unethical.

Confronted with this information, Emily saw how someone could perceive her behavior as dishonest. She also knew that without the formal feedback process, she probably never would have figured this out. What Emily learned prompted her to stop the practice and to go to extra lengths to explain when top management would override her decision on holding any piece of business. Subsequent feedback 6 months later showed improved integrity ratings. Emily's take-away was a lifelong commitment to asking for feedback.

## Discover a Victory

When a vice president of operations was asked what especially pleased him about the information he gleaned from his 10 direct reports in feedback surveys, he answered: "Definitely that item about positively recognizing people. Last year, that showed up as a real weakness, so I've worked hard on it." When feedback lets you know that the changes you have made are working and people's perceptions have changed, it is time to pat yourself on the back. Realizing the victory can be energizing and encourage continued efforts.

## Reveal Your Blind Spots

The world as seen through your lens probably has some large chunks of missing information in it.

### BLIND SPOT QUIZ

1. What one thing does your boss admire most about you?

2. What's the number one thing your administrative assistant would like you to do differently to help him or her work more effectively?

3. What are your top three leadership strengths, according to your team?

4. What is the most important thing you could improve right now to be a better leader to your direct reports?

5. How do your peers see you?

If you are confident in all your answers, you excel in collecting valuable information that can make you better in leadership and in business. However, if you are guessing, wondering how others would answer, you have some blind spots. If you have devised a plan for how to be a better leader based only on your own perceptions, you may not ever arrive. Give others the chance to help you. Ask for the information you need.

Susan Wise, an executive coach, helps her clients see what could be holding them back by drawing two concentric circles. The smaller inner circle represents a zone of comfort, and the area outside is one of discomfort. We all operate in our comfort zones, and for most successful leaders, most of what they do works well. Feedback brings possible new behaviors into focus, requiring one to reach into that uncomfortable zone. The zone of discomfort has strategies, beliefs, and skills that would further increase effectiveness but often are not used. With practice and subsequent success, those effective behaviors from the outside zone of discomfort will move into the comfort zone. Says Susan: "Leaders who don't open themselves for feedback are doomed to live forever with their blind spots."

## HOW TO ASK

Asking people for feedback does not have to be a formal exercise. Some leaders are great at making it part of their style, regularly seeking input through casual interactions.

Also recognize, however, that face-to-face requests for feedback can be awkward and problematic. If you seek feedback informally, you must come across as very authentic, you must not put others on the spot, and you must have high-trust relationships. Depending on your organization's culture and how much you are trusted by the person you are asking for information, they may wonder, "Can this information be used against me and hurt my career? Is there a hidden agenda? Can I trust that this will be used in the right way? Will I hurt his or her feelings or make him or her angry?"

**Of 5612 executives, 79 percent said that their leaders could do better at promoting open and sincere communication.**

Organizations that operate with the kind of open, safe culture required to have effective informal feedback are rare. Most leaders fall short of establishing such an atmosphere. Of 5612 executives, 79 percent said that their leaders could do better at promoting open and sincere communication.

When straightforwardness, honesty, and trust are not part of the culture or at least part of a leader's relationships with his or her direct reports, expecting people to suddenly feel comfortable with inquisitiveness may be unrealistic. However, if you are confident that the company's atmosphere or your relationships will allow for informal feedback, then determine a way to ask that is authentic and makes others comfortable. You might, for example, seek feedback about how you are doing at running effective staff meetings by asking your team for two things they like and two things they would change about your weekly meeting. You could give them the option of answering in a scheduled one-on-one conversation or by e-mail because some people are more comfortable in written formats. Give them time to test you and trust your intentions.

Also realize that in order to get meaningful information, you need specifics. In order to make an improvement, you have to know exactly which of your behaviors drive a certain person's perspective about you. Be prepared to ask questions that elicit the kinds of details you need:

❑ "Can you give me an example?"

❑ "What does it look like?"

❑ "When does it happen most?"

❑ "Tell me some more."

❑ "If it were on videotape, what would I look like?"

❑ "Show me."

If asking for feedback in this way does not feel right to you, don't do it. Find other leaders who have been successful at it, and talk to them. Take your time. If you want information from your team or family about how you can be a better leader, colleague, salesperson, father, CEO, or business partner, there are lots of options.

A process of formal feedback involving anonymous surveys and/or confidential interviews by an outside professional encourages conversations between the leader and individuals, as well as between the leader and the team. Assessment inventories can be customized to focus on specific issues or overall performance. Outside consultants can put the feedback into perspective and/or conduct confidential interviews to gain further information. Videoconferencing and phone coaching to review feedback are becoming more common and successful alternatives. Such survey instruments have even been developed for families. They can be extremely powerful exchanges and can change the nature of relationships forever. If done well, a formal feedback process can, over time, encourage an organizational culture that allows for safe and effective informal feedback.

Whether you pursue feedback informally or formally, you would be wise to consider the following:

*Don't ask during their performance review.* Reviews are a formal process of communicating important performance and career development information, and most employees yearn for this feedback from their bosses, especially if a leader does not provide regular feedback outside review time. However, even though your follower might appreciate that you want information about your performance in return, asking for it at the end of a review is terrible timing. Performance evaluations often are emotional experiences, and the employee will be focused on his or her development issues and his or her own career. It is *the employee's* review session, not yours. So ask another time.

*Clearly state why you are asking for feedback.* "I want to be a better CEO for this company, and I need your help in order to do that." Or, "I am developing a personal action plan to improve how I communicate with you all, and I need your input." Or, "I want to get better at making you all feel recognized and valued, and I'd like to know your opinions." Connect the dots. If people do not understand the purpose, they might not want to get involved. When people know why they are being asked for information, how it will be used, and what the benefits of answering are, they will be more likely to extend themselves and offer thoughtful and valuable feedback.

*Resist a litany list.* Ask for one to three things you do well and one to three that you could improve. You do not want to be so unstructured as to possibly invite a whine session. You want quality feedback, and you want balanced feedback.

*Give people time to think.* If you choose the informal route, realize that on-the-spot feedback is not usually the best approach. Make this a thoughtful, meaningful experience. Give people a week to devote time and focus on what is important to them and ultimately to you, too. Schedule a conversation or, if you must, exchange e-mails.

*When appropriate, announce your plans to ask for feedback.* Whether you intend to ask for feedback informally or through structured surveys, let your followers hear you announce your intentions at the same time. This eliminates those unproductive news wires that sound something like "Did you hear that Al asked Linda for some feedback? He didn't ask me. Did he ask you?" Although you will gather answers from each of your followers individually, asking for feedback all at once is more efficient and sends a clear message that the event is not a secret and that everyone is equally important.

Here is a script that many use with success:

> I want to work on being a better leader, and I need your help. I'd like for you to think of one to three things I do as your leader that you like and appreciate. Then I'd like for you to come up with one to three things I could do better to be a better leader to you. I can't promise I'll be willing or able to make all the changes you ask for, but I promise to seriously consider all of them. Your input will be important information for me as I create a developmental plan.

## HOW TO RESPOND

Sitting calmly and listening to what other people think of us might not be a picnic. Hearing something we disagree with introduces what psychologists call "the threat of dissonance," whereby we are at first confused and frustrated, and to reduce the frustration, we flee mentally from the situation by tuning out what the speaker is saying or by distorting it so we will not have to alter our perceptions. We do this unconsciously, not deliberately (*The Dynamics of Human Communication*, Michelle Tolela Myers and Gail Myers, New York, McGraw-Hill, 1973, p. 203).

We also will put up large walls to defend our self-image. Asked whether their leaders accept constructive feedback in a positive manner and without defensiveness, 76 percent of 7444 executives said that there is room for improvement, and 80 percent of those leaders' bosses agreed.

**Asked whether their leaders accept constructive feedback in a positive manner and without defensiveness, 76 percent of 7444 executives said that there is room for improvement, and 80 percent of those leaders' bosses agreed.**

If your listener senses defensiveness or otherwise unappreciative and arms-across-your-chest responses, the interaction likely will have an abrupt ending. Here are some examples of feedback-buster responses that you will want to avoid when you are receiving feedback:

1. I can't believe you feel like that.
2. This doesn't make sense.
3. Don't you think that's immature?
4. Wait a minute now.
5. Look at my side of it.
6. After all I've done for you.
7. But it's such a little thing.
8. This is ridiculous.
9. This makes me feel awful.
10. You obviously don't understand.

If you find yourself in a feedback situation where the information causes you to bristle, for whatever reason, simply say "Thank you" and move on. You can always choose to respond further after you have taken time to allow the emotions to subside and to think clearly about a smart follow-up strategy.

When you learn about something that is important to others, you may want to make a change in your leadership style. If so, commit to a plan and proper timing. For instance, if your team wants you to be more accessible and more of a coach and you want to accommodate their request but the entire southeast sales structure is in transition, you may need to put change off. Show that you value their feedback, acknowledge that you agree, and then promise that you will get together with them within 60 days to determine the next steps. Delaying action with good reason is okay. Just be sure to follow through.

Before committing to any change, however, make sure that you not only believe in it but that you also feel sure that it is even possible. Since our first anniversary, my husband and I have always had annual "summit meetings" to get information from each other about how we can improve our marriage. I tell him a few items he is doing well and a few he could change, and he does the same for me. Admittedly, there are moments when both of us have to dig deep so as not to respond defensively. It is tempting to say, "Whoa, wait a minute, excuse me, the reason I do that is . . . you don't understand." But usually we manage to resist the urge and get to the information that's important. One of the items on Herb's request list has been, "I'd appreciate it if you'd put things back where you find them. It would make life easier." He is not the kind of person who likes to hunt for the remote control. And he does not understand why it is difficult for me to return things to the same place I got them. When he first brought this request to the table, I told him that I would have to think about it. After a week, I went to him and said, "You know, I understand that this is important to you, but I can't do it." Remember, credibility is based on honesty with others, and that starts with being honest with yourself. I was not proud of this. I would have preferred to say, "Sure, I'll do that. Not a problem." But I know it is simply not in my makeup to be so neat, and promising otherwise would have set Herb up for a big disappointment and me up for failure. "I can't do it" can be an appropriate response to a request made through feedback, especially if it means that you maintain honesty and keep your promises.

Before you *do* anything in response to someone's feedback, think. Ask yourself

❑ Can I do this? Am I capable of it?

❑ Do I want to do it?

❑ Is this the right time?

Also consider the following to ensure that you respond effectively:

*Talk about the feedback.* If you have gone through a formal feedback process, have a personal conversation about your feedback, making a response evident to your followers or peers. Do not just casually mention it in the hallway or squeeze in a few comments before a Monday morning staff meeting. Address your team or sit with an individual and say something like, "I got my feedback. Thank you for taking the time to give me your thoughts. Now, I'd like to share what I learned." Summarize what you learned. Keep it brief and practical.

*Share the good news.* Tell others what you learned that you were glad to hear about. Assure them that you are going to keep doing all those things they appreciate.

*Take bold action.* If you want to make a change and the time is right, make the change obvious. Even consider announcing it. If you move too slowly with subtle changes, people may not notice anything different. If you are not going to make destructive comments anymore, say: "I won't be making destructive comments anymore, and if I slip up, please let me know." Of course, you would not want to take such bold action unless you firmly believed in the value of and your ability to make the change.

*Don't be overzealous.* Trying to change too many things at once is tempting for many high-achieving leaders. But remain focused. People probably will be content if you choose one thing to improve and you do so with great success. Target one or two things over the next 6 months, make a plan, and work it.

*Clearly define your target.* Change becomes nearly impossible if goals are not specific. "Be a better listener" is too loose, whereas "avoid interrupting others" is a specific behavior that can help you to listen more effectively.

*Follow up with people—again and again and again.* This is a critical step and one that most leaders fail to do. Follow up with your team individually at regular intervals—perhaps every 2 months. Doing so allows you to monitor your progress and possibly get additional information that might help you in the change process. Studies prove that the more consistent the follow-up, the more effective the leader is perceived to be. And consistent follow-up can result in perceptions of improvement not only in target areas but also in overall leadership effectiveness.

## PRAISE IS EQUALLY VALUABLE

I once asked a leader in his fifties why he had given himself the highest possible score in every indicator on an assessment. "I'm a politician," he said. "We always vote for ourselves." This man had a high regard for himself.

Usually, however, people are rather hard on themselves and consequently do not accept positive feedback well. When leaders are not good at receiving and accepting praise, the givers may feel slighted. These responses are vague denials of positive feedback:

❑ "It's nothing, really."

❑ "You're good at what you do, too."

❑ "Okay thanks, but let's move on to. . . ."

❑ "I was raised like that."

❑ "But that's my job."

These kinds of statements can sound as if the person is deflecting the positive feedback and diminishing the praise and even the person who offered it.

Truly accepting and internalizing the good grades is just as important as absorbing the constructive criticism. I have sat with stunned leaders as they read thoughtful, well-crafted comments like

❑ "Harvey is one in a million. I have the highest respect for his personal integrity and professionalism."

❑ "Brian honestly respects, appreciates, and values us and our work. He's simply the best boss I've ever had."

❑ "I have the ultimate respect for Christine. She should have her boss' job as soon as possible."

❑ "I truly believe there is nothing Linda can't accomplish, and I am honored to be a part of her team."

❑ "Steve is incredibly conscientious and considerate of others. He is a great team player. He is beloved by them."

While feedback is normally kept confidential, I have more than once suggested to a leader that he or she celebrate the good news with family. "Promise me that you will take this home and show your wife how lucky she is. Rip this page out and tape it on the fridge tonight. Everyone in your house needs to know this about you. Take a moment and read some of these comments again—maybe this weekend." They often think that I am being silly, but I am serious about giving positive admiration a second look, and often a successful leader is able to become that successful because there are people at home providing love, support, a hot meal, a pressed skirt or shirt, and a sensitive sounding board.

Turning a blind eye or skipping over the positives may result in your not fully understanding what's working. Some leaders say, "Let's just get to what I need to work on. That's the point of getting this feedback, isn't it?" No, not entirely. Knowing what you do well and what others appreciate are as valuable as your biggest criticism.

## THE COURAGE TO ASK

At a Delta Air Lines social gathering, I asked a commercial pilot who had flown in Vietnam to give me an example of a time in his career when he was forced to dig deep for courage.

"Well, you know, I have a lot to think about," he said. "Let me mull this over for about 30 minutes, and I'll get back to you."

Sure enough, he returned a little while later with his answer. I anticipated an awesome war story. What I got was this: "When I have just made one of the worst landings in my entire career and I then have to stand at the door of the aircraft and shake hands with 250 people who might just tell me what they thought of my performance, that takes tremendous courage. Sometimes I stay in the cockpit and tie my shoes two or three times to let the first 100 people walk out."

Not an exciting battle tale, but there is a good lesson in there. No matter how open to criticism we think we are, our egos never like to hear it. We like to be right, and we do not like to be challenged. When we are told something that is contrary to the beliefs we have about ourselves, we naturally become defensive. If you ask others for information about yourself, they might oblige. Can you handle it?

Leaders who stand forward, ask for feedback, and maybe even make a positive change gain respect and credibility through transparency. They also inspire others to do the same and promote a spirit of collaborative self-development. There is great power in simply asking others for input.

# ARE YOU GOOD AT ASKING FOR FEEDBACK?

Using the following scale, rate each expectation of credible leaders in two ways:

How well do you think you are doing at meeting the expectation?

What might others think about how well you are meeting the expectation?

**SCALE**: 1 = significant improvement needed; 2 = slight improvement needed; 3 = skilled/competent; 4 = talented; 5 = outstanding: a role model

| EXPECTATION | HOW DO YOU THINK YOU ARE DOING? | WHAT MIGHT OTHERS THINK? |
|---|---|---|
| Works to grow personally and professionally. | 1 2 3 4 5 | 1 2 3 4 5 |
| Regularly asks for feedback and suggestions to improve own performance. | 1 2 3 4 5 | 1 2 3 4 5 |
| Accepts constructive feedback from others in a positive manner (i.e., avoids defensiveness). | 1 2 3 4 5 | 1 2 3 4 5 |
| Listens actively and demonstrates an understanding of others' views and needs. | 1 2 3 4 5 | 1 2 3 4 5 |
| Sends message of "I'm not perfect" versus "I know it all." | 1 2 3 4 5 | 1 2 3 4 5 |
| Demonstrates accurate assessment of his or her strengths and developmental areas (i.e., has realistic self-awareness). | 1 2 3 4 5 | 1 2 3 4 5 |

Responds to and incorporates    1 2 3 4 5   1 2 3 4 5
feedback to make changes and
adjustments in behaviors when
appropriate.

**MY SCORES:**

*Scoring yourself:* Add your total for each column. A single column score of 31 to 35 suggests that you are doing an exceptional job and meeting others' expectations of someone who seeks out feedback. A column score of 26 to 30 indicates that you have some areas for improvement; on issues as important as these, I believe leaders should strive to be "outstanding: a role model." Below 26 indicates a danger area, and you may be chipping away at your credibility. A discrepancy of more than 8 points between the two column totals indicates a possible gap in perception worth investigating. If your "How do you think you are doing?" score is higher than your "What might others think?" score, your intentions may be better than your actions. If your "What might others think?" score is higher, you may not be giving yourself enough credit for a job well done.

# CHAPTER 4

# Compose Yourself

*I think the guys who are really controlling
their emotions . . . are going to win.*

—Tiger Woods

J ordan Fladell earned his nickname, "The Tornado," early in his career as a dot-com entrepreneur. Once, when employees did not fill out time sheets as they were expected to do, he gathered all 14 of the Internet startup's employees into a conference room after lunch, and while standing on the table with a 55-gallon plastic waste can, he yelled, "This is what happens when we don't fill out time sheets. We throw money away!" Then he tore up payroll checks (which were blank, although the employees did not know it), let the pieces float into the waste can, kicked the can down the hall, and yelled a little more before jumping off the table and storming out the door. Fladell's team, all silent and shocked, quietly dispersed, and some avoided him for days.

In his professional and personal life, Fladell has high expectations, a "no excuses" mantra, and a win-lose sports mentality that stems from years of playing football, baseball, and roller hockey and wrestling. All have helped him to become, at age 32, the cofounder and chief sales officer of Definition 6, an Atlanta-headquartered, Web-based consulting firm that, even after the dot-com bust, is in its fifth year of growth, with revenues near $6 million. His brash style of leadership, however, also brought a downside. Some employees were not entirely comfortable around Fladell, unsure of when the next tornado would hit.

Not long after the trashcan incident, Fladell went on a "screaming spree" after sales managers made a decision that he did not like while he was out of the office one day. Somehow the event hit home with him (no one would have dared call him on his behavior), and he realized that the way he was acting was wrong and felt that his personal integrity was at stake. "[The behavior] . . . was really in conflict with the way I believe others should be treated," Fladell admitted. After speaking with a couple of people in the company about the issue and being told that his "belligerent" behavior prevented results, he apologized to his staff in a company wide meeting and immediately began making positive changes.

"I still get upset, especially over customer issues, but now I take a deep breath, debrief with my partner, and follow the 'hot fire rule'—no matter how hot you get, you can't fire someone on the spot, you have to cool off and wait until the next day." Fladell believes that by not yelling and by being more "emotionally mature," he is allowing his employees to be more comfortable with him and more productive. He has worked on converting his energy to helping his subordinates reach their goals, and that strategy has been a winning one for everyone and the company. "When someone tells me I've made a difference in their career or their life, that's better than any sale or contract. That's the greatest victory for me."

At the core of Fladell's new wisdom is the idea that effective and admirable leadership requires composure. Challenges, stressors, and obstacles are inherent in any organization and in any leader's path; how a leader conducts himself or herself during the good times and the bad can be indicative of his or her character, competence, and ultimately, credibility. While the call for transparency that builds credibility urges leaders to reveal their true opinions and emotions regarding relevant business issues, it does not allow for leaders to irresponsibly let it all hang out. Especially during tough times, followers expect their leaders to be composed, calming, readying, and focusing the team.

However, you may be wondering: Isn't it better to be effective than composed? This is business, after all. I need bottom-line results, not a reputation for being calm and steady. Today you will have difficulty being effective without composure. It is a formula that even Microsoft has realized is necessary for success in today's business environment.

A November 2002 article in the *New York Times Magazine*, "Microsofter," describes the new personality that the company and its chief executive officer (CEO), Steve Ballmer, are trying to project: "older, wiser, calmer," and "transparent." Writer Steve Bodow explains that since its former Goliath's leverage has been weakened by a giant antitrust suit and increased competition, gone are the days when the company could "get away with simply being a bully." Ballmer, especially, is working on getting control of his brash, impulsive personality; he used to scream so much at sales meetings that he had to have surgery to repair his wasted vocal cords, and a once widely circulated video, tagged "Monkeyboy," showed the Microsoft executive rallying the troops "in ways that seemed, well, primal," according to Bodow. This reputation almost cost Ballmer his 2001 promotion to Bill Gates' former position because the company's board was concerned about his "hotheadedness" (*New York Times Magazine*, November 24, 2002, pp. 72–75).

A leader's composure should not be underestimated as a vital ingredient for long-term success. To be effective in influencing followers, to be well regarded (if not well liked), to be seen as credible, indeed *to be thought of as a leader*, one must possess a solid, steady, controlled demeanor during challenging, stressful, and emotionally charged times and exhibit "grace under fire," keeping followers focused on the vision and working toward a common purpose during periods of change or opposition.

## THROWN ANY OFFICE FURNITURE LATELY?

More than 60 years ago, my father rode a mine cart 2 miles underground 6 days a week to his 3-foot-high "room" where he would tap in his explosives, light the wire, and quickly crawl away, covering his ears as the blast unearthed coal. He was paid 72 cents a ton. And every time he emerged from the dark earth, he thanked God for letting him see the light of day one more time.

Stress is relative. One leader's requirement to let go of a half-dozen employees just before Christmas might be the worst challenge he or she has ever met. Another leader who is forced to face angry shareholders over a failed merger may think my father's coal mining days to be a walk in the park. But how well do leaders perform under the pressures inherent in any business? Of 2052 employees who participated in surveys, 68 percent said that their leaders could improve at working constructively under pressure, and 73 percent of those leaders' bosses agreed.

> **Of 2052 employees who participated in surveys, 68 percent said that their leaders could improve at working constructively under pressure, and 73 percent of those leaders' bosses agreed.**

In facing challenges large and small, emotions erupt. The best of leaders will experience anger, disgust, frustration, sadness, or fear at various points in their career. And yet the business world does not put out a welcome mat for emotions. Emotions are an integral part of personal relationships, but in the professional world we are told to avoid them or at least approach them cautiously, as if tiptoeing up to a roped-off crime scene.

Rescued in part by best-selling author Daniel Goleman, some organizations have embraced his concept of "emotional intelligence" and are now talking about feelings at work, recognizing that emotions are part of our professional lives, too. Emotional competency—one's EQ—is thought to be even more important than how smart you are when it comes to determining business success. Emotional intelligence—consisting of self-awareness, self-management, social awareness, and social skills—is the active ingredient in outstanding leaders, according to Goleman's research (*Emotional Intelligence*, by Daniel Goleman, New York, Bantam Books, 1995).

Allison, an inside sales manager for a telecommunications company, was plugging along at work one rainy Monday. It was "one of those days" when lots of little problems add up to a big, bad day. Allison knew that her Monday was not going well, but she did not pause to think about how she could turn it around. In fact, she completely ignored her emotions, which intensified as she pounded ahead. At midday Allison decided to attack her list of phone messages that needed to be returned, but the office phone system was overloaded. She could not get an outside line. Every time she tried to dial a number, she would get a fast busy signal. Frustrated, Allison slammed down the phone, cursed it with an expletive, and slapped her hand on the desk. Several of her direct reports looked on in shock. When did Allison start feeling her emotions getting the best of her? Was there a point at which she could have diffused the increasing intensity?

Managing your composure requires you to have a high degree of self-awareness—recognizing your feelings as they emerge and how certain reactions to those feelings may affect others. Think of a particular emotion on a continuum ranging from a low level of feeling to a high level of feeling. Take anger as an example.

**ANGER**

1 2 3 4 5 6 7 8 9 10

Low level of feeling                                 High level of feeling

Of course, some people never experience the "Anger" rating of 9 to 10. Some people just do not get that angry—it is not in their makeup. However, everyone feels anger at some level. And learning to express anger appropriately, especially when the intensity is in the 7 to 10 range, increases your composure rating. Allison, for example, probably was only experiencing anger in the 5 to 6 range, but given the day she was having, it got the best of her. Consequently, she lost her composure—all because she could not get an outside line to place a telephone call.

Building leadership credibility through composure is not about controlling your emotions, but rather, it is about controlling your *reactions* to emotions. However, high levels of emotion can overwhelm good judgment and reduce the possibility of a successful outcome. You must react to those feelings—even the good ones, such as elation and surprise—in a way that shows your emotional maturity. When voices raise, fingers point, eyes bulge, or tears spill, onlookers want to distance themselves. They lower their eyes, suddenly become engrossed in their work, or try to appear nonchalant as they gather up a few files and head out. Witnesses to frustration and anger usually experience a degree of discomfort and embarrassment. They may even pity the coworker or boss who loses control.

And "losing it" is not an uncommon occurrence among leaders. When asked whether their boss displays a high degree of composure or emotional maturity, more than 60 percent of 2118 executives said that improvement was in order, and 73 percent of those leaders' bosses agreed.

> **When asked whether their boss displays a high degree of composure or emotional maturity, more than 60 percent of 2118 executives said that improvement was in order, and 73 percent of those leaders' bosses agreed.**

Many executives are surprised that composure is a significant factor in determining credibility. Indeed, its impact on a person's reputation is often underestimated, and people seem to assume that others will understand what they are going through and forgive their weak moments. Yet our composure is measured every day by our peers, boss, customers, and direct reports as they interact with us and watch how we handle ourselves. And it is often with the less significant stressors—the everyday challenges and casual interactions—that we lose a high composure rating, the times when we might not realize we are on stage.

## GOOD MENTAL HYGIENE

Try to project yourself into the following situations:

❏ A colleague shoots down your idea for a marketing campaign in front of your boss. What do you say?

❏ You are disappointed by what you feel is an unfair performance review. How do you react?

❏ An explicit joke makes you uncomfortable. How do you respond?

❏ Your boss suddenly informs you that he needs you to work during the week of your family vacation that has been planned for 6 months. How do you handle it?

Every situation, even the seemingly insignificant interactions, offers an opportunity to choose behaviors that enhance or diminish a composure rating.

The key to keeping your cool is to become less reactive and impulsive in your interactions with others. You have to keep your emotional brain from overpowering your thinking brain. Leaders can identify, using the preceding continuum of emotions, the level at which they know they become close to reacting in a way that might seem less than composed. When, in their day-to-day interactions with others, they reach that level on the emotional continuum, they should train themselves to flip an internal switch that says, "Be calm and be careful."

Consider adopting one or all of the following actions to remain composed during emotional highs:

1. *Put some air in your lungs.* People who meditate concentrate on their breathing to remain focused, calm, and centered. You don't have to be a yogi to experience the same benefits.

2. *Wait a minute.* You can even say, "I need a moment to think about this." Doing so not only gives you time to choose a reaction (instead of being impulsive), but it also alerts those around you that the situation deserves your full attention.

3. *Think "slow and low."* Before you say a word, choose your voice level. In difficult moments, opt for a low and well-modulated tone, and speak more slowly than usual.

4. *Imagine what others might be feeling.* This not only helps you choose an intelligent response, but it also moves the focus away from what you are feeling and could diminish some of the intensity of your emotion.

5. *Frame a response without "red flag" words.* While emotions are peaking, it is best to choose bland, safe language. Stay away from loaded words such as *always, never, stupid,* or *ridiculous,* which tend to weaken your points, not strengthen them.

6. *Consider putting off a resolution.* Communication laden with emotion rarely produces good solutions. If you can, take time to collect yourself before resolving the situation. If a decision has to be made immediately, consider asking, "What do you think should happen?" It is not only inclusive, but it could generate an option you may not have thought about.

Also be aware that a lack of composure is indicated not only in overreactions to emotions but also in frequent mood shifts. A Seattle police chief had a sign on his desk that said, "My Mood Changes Without Notice," and according to his direct reports, this was indeed true. If they had to bring him bad news, sometimes he reacted with, "Thank you very much for letting me know," and other times he would blow up.

What do you think people will say about you if

| ON SOME DAYS YOU . . . | ON OTHER DAYS YOU . . . |
| --- | --- |
| Insist on doing things one way. | Do things differently. |
| Compliment colleagues. | Badmouth them. |
| Encourage long, chatty interludes. | Abruptly cut people off. |
| Let deadlines or punctuality slide. | Explode when someone is late. |
| Joke and tease. | Growl and sulk. |

They probably will call you something like "moody" or "unpredictable." Different behavior from one day to another confuses people, even unnerves them, and inconsistency can breed doubt and distrust. People do not like to be surprised all the time when it comes to a leader's moods. A degree of predictability and consistency in behavior is preferred.

## TOO MUCH OF A GOOD THING

Which of the following situations could cause someone to be perceived as lacking composure?

1. As CEO, Tricia feels strongly that her company should make every effort to fill a vacant position for a senior officer with a minority person. When the executive in charge of the search brings Tricia the narrowed list of candidates' profiles, she quickly sees that none are minorities, shoves the papers back, and glares. "Don't you get it? There's not a woman or an African-American on this list."

2. At a quarterly meeting with all 300 employees, the president recognizes the company's unprecedented increase in revenues due to the sales team's victory in landing a huge account against the odds. He asks the team to stand, and while the audience applauds excitedly and some sales members high-five each other, one member whistles through his fingers and beats his chest while doing a Tarzan call.

If you thought both could be damaging, you are right. Even overreactions to positive or seemingly harmless emotions can decrease one's composure rating.

Jeanne Walsh, senior vice president of special projects for the Eastern Division of the American Cancer Society, is obviously passionate about fighting cancer. She loves her work, and she is a ball of fire—perky and smart, with a track record of making good decisions from her gut. Walsh's creativity and ability to inspire volunteers have resulted in strategic international partnerships that have made a difference to people fighting the disease, and her coworkers like and admire her except for one thing: "She can be way too out there with her emotions," a colleague said. Another said: "She's as good as they get, but this hurts her professionally." Walsh's high standards, including a zealous belief in fairness and compassion for the cause, sometimes produce high-flying emotions and impulsive reactions. Once she was so furious with a decision her boss was making that she hung up on a conference call.

Personally, Walsh was concerned about how she was coming across but also struggled with whether a change meant she would have to be less authentic. "I feel like I'm going to have to change who I really am, and that bothers me," she said. But tinkering around with the essence of Jeanne was not what composure was about, and she learned that there are strategies that can help her remain composed without changing her core nature.

For instance, Walsh looked at how she could handle an upcoming conference call on a sensitive issue. In the past she would just barrel right in and react to the topic, but this time she didn't. Instead, she listened, asked questions, and took notes, starring items that she felt really strongly about. After the call, she put together a well-thought-out memo to her boss and the CEO outlining a strategy for resolving the issues.

Despite reservations in the beginning, Walsh now works hard to monitor and regulate her emotions. "I can definitely see now how my emotions were affecting how people viewed me," she said. "It's not easy, but now I feel more in control, and I think others see it too."

Can too much energy have a downside? Can you be *too* happy or *too* excited? These comments from leadership surveys reveal how too much of a good thing can be perceived negatively:

❑ "Temper your passion and optimism. It gets in your way sometimes."

❑ "Jim is a high-energy leader. He brings enthusiasm to the team. But his credibility suffers when he has emotional responses to staff. Others sometimes see him as being unstable."

❏ "Katy's voice tone is very loud and gets to be annoying. As she gets more excited, her voice tone increases. Needs to work on this."

❏ "Do not get emotional over an issue. Matter-of-fact communication is most effective. His passion at times can be misunderstood."

❏ "Joanna needs to tone down her the-sky-is-falling vibes. She needs to approach her work in a calmer demeanor as she tends to create unnecessary anxiety with peers and subordinates."

Positive emotions can be applied to the emotional continuum as well. If your excitement, happiness, or passion reaches a level where you might react in a way that lacks composure, take a minute and choose your behaviors wisely. Gloating over a promotion can be just as damaging as losing your cool under pressure.

## GRACE UNDER FIRE

When Susan Williams was vice president for administration and planning at Belmont University in Nashville, she observed then-President Bill Troutt as he was faced with significant opposition from the faculty, staff, and students around proposed changes. It was the early 1990s, the private university was beginning a continuous improvement initiative, and Troutt advocated improvement in the way the university did its business. "He gave a speech that essentially said, 'the train's headed in this direction, I want you to go, but if you don't get on board, you'll probably be going somewhere else,'" recalled Williams, who is now a professor in Belmont's graduate business program and one of the nation's nine judges for the Malcolm Baldridge National Quality

Award, a 3-year post appointed by the Secretary of Commerce. "But rather than saying, 'these are the tablets from the top of the mountain, and this is what we're doing no matter what you think,' he asked members of the university community for their opinion and got them involved," Williams said. Troutt asked for input both informally and formally through a survey that asked all students, staff, and faculty: What delights you about Belmont? What disappoints you? If you could change one thing, what would it be? Williams said that there was a response rate of approximately 90 percent. From their input came initiatives that eventually changed the fabric of Belmont. The process of change was largely successful because the organization's leader knew how to build coalitions in the face of opposition. Although Troutt had been firm in his direction from the start, Williams said, he also recognized that people usually support what they help to create.

Leaders today are waist deep in challenges, and at some point in their careers, most CEOs, business owners, and senior executives must lead their organizations through a crisis of change. A leader known to have "grace under fire" earns it and likely has scar tissue to prove it. When alligators are staring back at you, here are some things to keep in mind:

*Be front and center.* In times of upheaval, a leader's visibility is paramount. Former New York City mayor Rudolph Giuliani was on the scene at the World Trade Center within minutes of the first terrorist attack, and in the weeks that followed September 11, 2001, he seemed to be everywhere—twice-daily press conferences, funerals, and memorial services. When the challenge hits, ask yourself: Who needs to see me? The people in your organization, department, or team want to see their leader—the captain—not just the flight attendants. Maintain high visibility by getting out of your office, touring facilities, and meeting with people. Answer their questions and keep them as informed as possible while also making clear that a course of action will soon be clear. "Let's stay focused on what we can control, not what we can't. Let's be patient until we get all the facts."

*Remind them of their purpose.* President Bush urged Americans to get back to their normal life routines after 9/11 and also urged everyone to help through their local charities. A lack of direction can create more tension, so leaders need to point people toward a meaningful target during tough times. Consider revisiting the organization's values, vision statement, and guiding principles with people to give a sense of purpose.

*Ask for help.* Too often those at the top of an organization feel that they alone are capable of figuring out the pathway out of disaster. In certain situations, going it alone may be the only way; and ultimately, leaders are responsible for the decisions made. However, involving others may reveal a better plan of action. And as Bill Troutt proved, getting the troops involved is an effective way to build support and enthusiasm.

*Give directions over and over.* Clear, pointed information dispels confusion and worry. Do not let people free-float during a crisis. Once a plan is determined, craft a simple message that reminds people of the target, and deliver it frequently.

*Show tough empathy.* In a crisis, a leader must be calm and rational—staying focused on the task at hand—while still conveying care and respect for individuals. Leaders who take the unbalanced "stiff upper lip" approach probably will not connect with people who are experiencing fear, uncertainty, anger, or disappointment. Consequently, those who lead from the head and the heart are likely to be more effective.

*Set the pace.* Drastic changes can hit even the most composed executive right in the gut, yet leaders are expected to remain calm, point the way, and set the pace. When faced with a problem, many managers move into action. They adopt a tactic of attack, and when that tactic runs into problems, they move to another tactic—and another and another—without slowing enough to analyze what went wrong in the first place. Choose wise action over incessant activity. When we operate at full speed ahead, our decision making may not be at its best. Complex issues may require time. Also keep in mind that leaders who consistently present themselves as hurried can make followers uneasy and anxious. Business is inherently stressful, but a harried leader can feed the frenzy. People who are frequently rushed are described in these ways:

❏ "When work gets busy, she gets very fanatic with her management skills. The staff tends to get the brunt of her anxiousness in the form of impatience, ineffective/inconsistent communication, and the transference of her stress to us."

❏ "Meetings are scheduled on top of one another, which doesn't leave time for her to breathe and organize herself for other meetings. When the department needs to talk to her, or she needs us, it's usually in between these tightly scheduled meetings. If only she'd slow down. Right now we aren't getting the best of Donna."

❏ "If Bruce could slow down—or at least pretend to— we'd gain a better leader."

❏ "You're always in crisis management mode, and you need to slow down."

❏ "You can be brusque when busy and stressed."

## CHOOSING COMPOSURE

It is during the tough times that being a steady, purposeful, and calm leader is such a challenge. Oddly, emotional overreactions are sometimes an attempt to regain control of a situation. At the time, yelling orders at the troops can seem like the best, most effective choice, no matter how stupid and ill-conceived it may appear later.

Leaders with high composure ratings in 360-degree assessments are described as being "patient, even under pressure," maintaining an "even keel," never losing their temper, and appearing "calm and cool in high-stress situations." You should aim for similar targets. Provide direction like a dignified general, for although followers will appreciate a leader's transparency—especially in uncertain times—the leader must express and reveal himself or herself with purpose and a sense of control, maintaining a solid, steady demeanor.

## ARE YOU A COMPOSED LEADER?

Using the following scale, rate each expectation of credible leaders in two ways:

How well do you think you are doing at meeting the expectation?

What might others think about how well you are meeting the expectation?

**SCALE:** 1 = significant improvement needed; 2 = slight improvement needed; 3 = skilled/competent; 4 = talented; 5 = outstanding: a role model

| EXPECTATION | HOW DO YOU THINK YOU ARE DOING? | WHAT MIGHT OTHERS THINK? |
|---|---|---|
| Shows a high degree of emotional maturity (e.g., composure, awareness). | 1 2 3 4 5 | 1 2 3 4 5 |
| Responds constructively when confronted with opposition or hostility. | 1 2 3 4 5 | 1 2 3 4 5 |

| | | |
|---|---|---|
| Exhibits "grace under fire." | 1 2 3 4 5 | 1 2 3 4 5 |
| Is predictable; mood does not change without notice. | 1 2 3 4 5 | 1 2 3 4 5 |
| Manages his or her anger, disappointment, and frustration positively. | 1 2 3 4 5 | 1 2 3 4 5 |
| Tempers passion and optimism when appropriate. | 1 2 3 4 5 | 1 2 3 4 5 |
| Is patient and unhurried in a fast-paced environment. | 1 2 3 4 5 | 1 2 3 4 5 |

**MY SCORES:**

*Scoring yourself:* Add your total for each column. A single column score of 31 to 35 suggests that you are doing an exceptional job and meeting others' expectations of someone who is composed. A column score of 26 to 30 indicates that you have some areas for improvement; on issues as important as these, I believe leaders should strive to be "outstanding: a role model." Below 26 indicates a danger area, and you may be chipping away at your credibility. A discrepancy of more than 8 points between the two column totals indicates a possible gap in perception worth investigating. If your "How do you think you are doing?" score is higher than your "What might others think?" score, your intentions may be better than your actions. If your "What might others think?" score is higher, you may not be giving yourself enough credit for a job well done.

# CHAPTER 5

# Let Your Guard Down

*For God's sake, choose a self and stand by it.*

—William James, OLDER BROTHER
OF NOVELIST HENRY JAMES

I f Al Stubblefield, chief executive officer (CEO) of Baptist Health Care (BHC), which ranked tenth on *Fortune*'s 2002 list of the nation's "Best Companies to Work For," mispronounces a name or makes a mistake using his "Mississippi math," he is likely the first to laugh. "I pick at myself and have fun with my mistakes," he says. Reminiscent of the colorful antics of retired Southwest Airlines CEO Herb Kelleher, Stubblefield once dressed in full football gear, "tight pants and all," for a Super Bowl–themed quarterly meeting with 500 of BHC's leaders and did "a respectable impromptu touchdown dance" on stage. He has also been a cowboy who "herded" several employees dressed up like cows.

Stubblefield tries hard to create a "collegial" environment and wants to be out among BHC staff ("not down to them"), far from the high and mighty CEO image. In fact, he is described by his staff as a leader who is "real," "approachable," and "down to earth" and "really makes you feel like he's listening to you."

A more personal side comes across in the stories Stubblefield tells in group and one-on-one interactions. That he lost 40 pounds last year was a topic. And he tells about what's going on with his four kids and his wife. The whole family sings in his church choir, and Stubblefield has been known to invite BHC executives to Sunday service. Recently, he and his brother, a doctor in Mississippi, challenged each other to read the whole Bible in a year, and he is not afraid to share a piece of scripture with his officers if he feels it "speaks to him" and says something meaningful about a current situation at work. If anyone gets offended by Stubblefield reading Bible verses in a work setting, they might be missing his point: "It gives them a sense of my spiritual depth and what's important to me," he says. "It's what makes me tick."

Reflecting on his leadership since the September 11, 2001 terrorist attacks and the string of national corporate scandals, Stubblefield believes that he probably has been more deliberate about showing his personal values and accentuating BHC's organizational values. "When I feel good about my pastor, I want to do things over and above showing up at church every Sunday." Similarly, if BHC employees understand that Stubblefield is "rock solid" in his values, "they'll probably run a little harder and come up with a couple more bright ideas to help take us to the next level."

Leaders who show their humanness and allow people to develop a strong understanding of who they really are can close the distance between themselves and their followers, strengthening work relationships and building credibility. Ultimately, followers cannot truly trust leaders unless they have some sense of who the leaders are, what's important to them, and what they stand for. Followers develop this sense when leaders are transparent enough to reveal themselves personally, showing their beliefs, perspectives, values, interests, and background.

Yet the personal authenticity part of leadership transparency is not as easy as Stubblefield's story might make it seem. Woe to the CEO who tries to build trust and good relationships by just letting it all hang out.

## THE PROBLEM WITH AUTHENTICITY

The late literary critic Lionel Trilling wrote that the virtue of simple sincerity had become devalued by a modern compulsion to be authentic, which seems to denote "a more strenuous moral experience" (*Sincerity and Authenticity*, Boston, Harvard University Press, 1972). Authenticity's popularity has indeed spread like a virus in all aspects of society but especially in business and politics. The ability to master this art of "just being yourself" has become a hot commodity.

And therein lies the problem. What began as a call for authentic self-expression in many ways became masterful strategizing to *appear* authentic. Politicians don plaid flannel shirts and employ just-an-average-guy rhetoric, and wealthy business owners drive Ford trucks to work, leaving their Porsches in the garage—attempts to present a just-folks authenticity. And while everyone has been trying to epitomize authenticity and give the illusion that what you see is what you get, society has sniffed out some fakes. In the wake of political and corporate scandals, we have become more discerning than ever and more capable of spotting engineered authenticity.

Those who have been caught up in appearances have in some ways muddied the water that holds the argument for authenticity in the first place. Authenticity is no more a congeniality contest than it is justification for authentic jerks to remain so. "Sorry, that's just the way I am."

From an organizational standpoint, *authenticity*—the congruence of our inner and outer selves—is about increasing trust, improving relationships, and solidifying values that hopefully create a meaningful context in which to do business.

Leaders who keep in mind the spirit of authenticity while working hard to create meaningful connections with their followers, demonstrating sincerity of being, and revealing personal information that adds value to the context of work will be practicing an important part of leadership transparency that builds credibility. Doing so, however, requires a certain level of maturity and self-awareness and a heightened sense of how people might perceive, dissect, and disseminate the information that you reveal. And because authenticity or personal transparency ultimately describes the quality of a relationship (one cannot be transparent unless one has someone to be transparent to), leaders must create opportunities in which to engage with their followers, allowing them to know their leaders.

## DECIDING WHAT'S IMPORTANT

Dr. Ron B. Goodspeed, president and CEO of Southcoast Hospitals Group in Fall River, Massachusetts, with three facilities and 5000 employees, offers an "owner's manual" on himself to those who work for him and anyone thinking about working for him. The manual, based on a self-assessment and input from associates, outlines the 56-year-old Goodspeed's leadership assets and warns of his shortcomings—like resorting to statistics and research data when uncomfortable with an idea, a tendency to ramble, and his penchant for analogies that sometimes muddy communication. Now given to all employees, the manual was written originally to help a new vice president "manage up." That new vice president said that his respect for Goodspeed "went up a notch" when he was given the manual, and he intends to write one on himself for his own direct reports ("Job Candidates Receive Some Tips on the Boss," by Joann S. Lubin, *Wall Street Journal*, January 7, 2003). Goodspeed clearly understands the importance of letting his people know what he is about and what makes him tick.

What should a leader include in his or her "owner's manual"? What information, whether revealed through Goodspeed's method or through daily interactions, adds value, creates trust, and helps to build a collaborative culture? Much depends on who you are, what you are comfortable with, and what you believe your organization's culture will tolerate. What would you like to keep private? What might happen if your team knew

❏ Your religious beliefs?

❏ Your political beliefs?

- ❏ Your views on pornography?

- ❏ Your child's drug problem?

- ❏ Your personal goals?

- ❏ Your most embarrassing moment?

- ❏ Your unfulfilled desires?

- ❏ Your major weakness?

- ❏ Your worries?

- ❏ Your biggest strengths?

- ❏ Whether you are happy with your life?

Authenticity does not require that you share intimate information about yourself and bare your soul. It does, however, demand that a leader sometimes stray from business-only conversations and share personal information—his or her lessons, beliefs, family life, and background.

Revealing personal challenges can underscore a leader's humanness, making him or her seem approachable and genuine, and exposing underdeveloped sides can help shatter the myth that a leader has all the answers. No one expects or wants perfection from a leader—then why would he or she need help from followers? Some experts advocate exposing a weakness as a means of protection, arguing that if you do not show a weakness, observers likely will invent one for you. While this is probably true, being so strategic with your weaknesses seems manipulative. The same can be true with the approach of choosing a weakness that can be considered a strength. "I'm a workaholic," for example, is arguably not a weakness and may sound contrived and insincere.

Revealing your trouble spots is tricky. You want to appear humble and human, not ill-suited for the job. Consider the new president of a university who, when asked questions about the school's finances in meetings with his executive team, says: "I really don't understand that budget yet." One of his direct reports told me that trust was eroding as he persistently revealed his lack of interest and lack of knowledge.

Highly personal information also should be handled carefully. Earlier in her career, as a vice president at a mail service company, Margaret received an unexpected phone call from her college-aged son who revealed to his mother that he was depressed and suicidal. Margaret quickly realized that she would need to take time to address her son's crisis. She did not think twice about walking into her boss's office to explain the situation and assure him that she would be on top of her work.

"From that moment on, our relationship changed," she said, "He saw me differently—not as his competent direct report but as a mother with a problem." She juggled her workload and her family priority for 6 months before things got better. Looking back, Margaret feels that she was not given assignments and that her career stalled for a while, even though she maintained her work responsibilities. If she had it to do over again, she would have done her work and kept quiet about her son's problem. "Another boss might have been different. I just don't think he was really capable of handling the information."

Leaders struggle with whether to share personal information at work. Those who do generally experience more positive results than negative, but how does a leader determine the risks? If you are concerned that revealing a particularly sensitive weakness or personal challenge might do more harm than good, ask yourself the following questions:

*What is my motivation?* The information ultimately should add value. Does it teach a lesson or help someone understand something? Does it help show empathy? Might it inspire change? If so, sharing it is worth considering.

*Is this the right time and place?* You do not want to walk away from a situation and think, "I wish I hadn't said that." Sensitive information could be misinterpreted or mistreated if it is not revealed in the proper context.

*Can this person handle the information?* This is ultimately a test of instincts. You should consider whether the person is trustworthy and mature enough to treat your information and you with respect.

## OPINIONS THAT MATTER

A senior executive at a large cable company, Karen, presented to her team information that she had received from the top about an organizational restructuring. Karen simply gave the facts, and her team was left to wonder: What does she think about the changes? Does she believe in the new structure? Where does she think the biggest challenge will be? Does she have concerns about the future?

Leaders who get caught up in being the mouthpiece of the organization can create a barrier between themselves and their teams. Relaying information from the top is commonly done robot-style. Karen's direct reports knew that they would not get every detail about the behind-the-scenes meeting, but they wanted to know what their leader thought about the reorganization.

Karen did not understand how important her opinions were to her team. Also, she felt that she could not reveal her personal analysis or viewpoints because the executive management team wanted to project a united front. Yet there were ways she could have offered insights while still being supportive of upper management. She could have said: "I struggled with that part in the beginning but came to see it in a different way." Or, "This part of the plan might cause some pain, but I think it's for the best."

Many times when I ask employees how their leader can be more effective, they say how "revealing yourself and what's on your mind" is important to them. In leadership assessments, people write

❑ "Express your opinions more. You are too quiet."

❑  "Larry should share more of his thoughts and ideas with us. He sometimes tends to sit back."

❑  "You're cheating us by not sharing your knowledge."

❑  "I've worked with her for a year and still don't feel like I know her. Will the real Susan please stand up?"

Through most of his 30-year career, Gary Burd, senior vice president of business practices at the American Cancer Society's Eastern Division, successfully connected with people and built strong relationships with his peers and followers. However, when a triple bypass forced him to reconsider his energy output, Burd focused on the necessary tasks, got complacent about his work relationships, and was content to sit back quietly in meetings. In a 360-degree survey, what Burd calls a "big wakeup call," he learned that people wanted to hear more of his thoughts and opinions and thought that he could work harder to cultivate relationships with them. "I can do that," Burd thought out loud in our coaching session. "Why am I not doing that?"

Burd's plan for improvement included doing things like scheduling one-on-one meetings with peers to exchange ideas, adding an extra 30 minutes to appointments at other American Cancer Society locations so that he could casually stop by people's offices, sitting next to different people at the senior executive dinners that were held every 2 months, making phone calls to peers to ask for their opinions on new projects he was creating, and during internal meetings, intentionally sharing his ideas and opinions. Not long after he began enacting the plan, Burd was a little preoccupied at a particular meeting and did not say much. Afterwards, one of his colleagues said to him, "Gary, we didn't hear from you today. Are you okay?"

"Sounds like they like the new you," I said to Burd. In fact, his boss, the organization's CEO, had already acknowledged that he and others liked the changes they were seeing.

One newly appointed vice president of customer care for a consumer products company was widely regarded as very intelligent and as having a wealth of industry knowledge.

"Nobody knows the business better than Kim," the company's vice president of operations said. Yet Kim's peers revealed in a 360-degree assessment that they did not fully trust her and were not confident about her as a team member. Even her boss was questioning his having promoted her to the position.

Kim's problem stemmed mostly from her lack of willingness to speak up in meetings, share her knowledge, and reveal her thoughts on issues. According to her team and boss, Kim would sit in an entire meeting and say nothing.

"Why are you doing that? Surely you have opinions," she was asked.

"Well, first of all, I am more of a listener. And second, why should I say something just for the sake of saying something?"

Not only was Kim quiet about business issues, she also was not sharing personal information either.

"Do you take time to talk with people about yourself and your family? What you enjoy doing?"

"There's not much to say really. We live pretty quiet."

Kim's quiet and reserved nature was hurting her peer relationships. Leaders who do not exchange information and share their knowledge, thoughts, and opinions do not own up to the reciprocal agreement in the relationship—it is a give and take. Like Kim, you may be shy or not understand how withholding information shuts off other people. Often we have certain ways of thinking that can keep us from wanting to share about our life outside work. Do you have these thoughts?

❏ I feel that it is important to keep my work life separate from my personal life.

❏ I am a very private person.

❏ I respect their privacy; they should respect mine.

❏ We are here to work together, not to be friends.

❏ I do not want to waste the company's time on chitchat.

Listening has always been touted as a vital leadership skill, but talking can be underrated. A mind set that reflects a work–personal life dichotomy makes it difficult to see value in engaging with people and sharing your personal side; but you cannot simply park your personality at the door. As leaders learn and grow, they should push their knowledge downward, sharing their secrets for success, grasp of the industry, and hard-won lessons. Followers usually want to hear them. Certainly this puts the onus on leaders to know their story— and share their story.

## DO YOU LET OTHERS KNOW YOU?

Using the following scale, rate each expectation of credible leaders in two ways:

How well do you think you are doing at meeting the expectation?

What might others think about how well you are meeting the expectation?

**SCALE**: 1 = significant improvement needed; 2 = slight improvement needed; 3 = skilled/competent; 4 = talented; 5 = outstanding: a role model

| EXPECTATION | HOW DO YOU THINK YOU ARE DOING? | WHAT MIGHT OTHERS THINK? |
|---|---|---|
| Is available and approachable, inviting conversation. | 1 2 3 4 5 | 1 2 3 4 5 |
| Demonstrates appropriate boundaries when sharing thoughts and feelings. | 1 2 3 4 5 | 1 2 3 4 5 |
| Shares personal information willingly when appropriate. | 1 2 3 4 5 | 1 2 3 4 5 |

| | | |
|---|---|---|
| Chooses the right time and place for sharing personal information. | 1 2 3 4 5 | 1 2 3 4 5 |
| Is professional yet authentic; presents the "real" person. | 1 2 3 4 5 | 1 2 3 4 5 |
| Makes time for small talk. | 1 2 3 4 5 | 1 2 3 4 5 |
| Engages in social situations, such as office events, lunches, and spontaneous interactions like stopping by a coworker's office. | 1 2 3 4 5 | 1 2 3 4 5 |

**MY SCORES:**

*Scoring yourself:* Add your total for each column. A single column score of 31 to 35 suggests that you are doing an exceptional job and meeting others' expectations of someone who makes personal connections through authenticity. A column score of 26 to 30 indicates that you have some areas for improvement; on issues important as these, I believe leaders should strive to be "outstanding: a role model." Below 26 indicates a danger area, and you may be chipping away at your credibility. A discrepancy of more than 8 points between the two column totals indicates a possible gap in perception worth investigating. If your "How do you think you are doing?" score is higher than your "What might others think?" score, your intentions may be better than your actions. If your "What might others think?" score is higher, you may not be giving yourself enough credit for a job well done.

## MAKING THE CONNECTIONS

Mark Albion, a former Harvard Business School professor and author of the *New York Times* best-selling book, *Making a Life, Making a Living* (New York, Warner, 2000), tells the story of David Rockefeller, former CEO of Chase Manhattan Bank, flying off to Saudi Arabia each month to visit a particular client for lunch, a cup of tea, or often, because the client was so busy, only a few moments of conversation before Rockefeller would return to New York. Asked why he did not just make a phone call or plan the trip so that he could spend more time with the client, Rockefeller explained: "I want him to know how important he is to our bank and to me personally. I will continue to visit him every month" ("P2P: Person to Person," by Mark Albion, *Fast Company*, August 2000).

Leaders who work hard to make personal connections with followers are taking a necessary step toward personal transparency—engaging others. Followers likely will not have the chance to know the "real person" unless their leader interacts with them. Although leaders may have many opportunities to engage with people, many often do not see value in casual conversations or friendly banter. Indeed, some move briskly down hallways, too intense about their work to take the time or make an effort even to say hello. These leaders are missing important opportunities to build trust. "Social skill is friendliness with a purpose," says Daniel Goleman, author of *Emotional Intelligence* (New York, Bantam, 1997). Leaders who engage and share themselves and their humanness often gain respect and loyalty and create caring and productive work communities.

In the small town of Pensacola, Florida, where Network Telephone is headquartered, employees are likely to see Chairman and CEO Ray Russenberger and his wife, Valerie, entertaining in the square, where the city hosts summer concerts; he plays the guitar and piano, and she sings.

Russenberger's employees also know that he is one of Pensacola's most successful self-made business owners. Prior to starting Network Telephone, an Internet and telephone service provider, he spent 13 years building a national paging company that was twice named as one of *Inc.* magazine's "500 Fastest Private Companies" in the country. He eventually sold it, made a bundle, and has been growing Network Telephone ever since. He speaks openly about his humble beginnings—he has no college degree and once spent 6 years paying creditors after his first attempt at starting a business ended in failure. Russenberger also makes no bones about his lack of attention to detail, a weakness he believes that he should make clear to those with whom he works. One of the first things he told his new administrative assistant was, "Never give me an original of anything." And to his executive team: "I'm not the person to ask for help on the details of a plan." They also know not to expect him to be around on Wednesday afternoons; for the last 15 years, that time has been reserved for his five children. "People have to observe your value system," he said. "You can't just talk about it." Although a little shy, Russenberger understands the importance of interacting with the 650 people of his organization not only while at work but also in social settings such as company barbeques or more spontaneous after-work gatherings. He is described by people as "one of us," and employees trust that what Russenberger believes is good strategy for the company is also good for their future, too.

Creating personal connections with people is not about being bosom buddies. It is about allowing for opportunities to be transparent in a personal way, a way that reveals who you are and what you are really about. And a leader has to make time for those opportunities. Kathleen Holmgren, senior vice president of Sun Microsystem's Network Storage Marketing Group, combines exercise with one-on-one sessions with her 12 direct reports. If you want to schedule time with Holmgren, bring your walking shoes. "I find that by getting out from behind the desk and going outside for a walk, not only do you get the business issues addressed, but you have a chance to really talk to them and get to know them better," she said. Holmgren, who has been with Sun for 18 years, is part of the network services company's Leadership Institute, an honor that indicates that she is in line to serve on CEO Scott McNealy's staff. Sun had $12.5 billion in 2002 revenues and has 39,000 employees worldwide.

Connecting with followers through personal transparency does not require that you have some kind of aura or charisma. In leadership assessments, people's comments indicate how it is the small things they appreciate:

❏ "Refreshingly approachable leader."

❏ "She understands our human side."

❏ "Doesn't treat you like an employee."

❏ "Greets us, engages in conversation, reflecting interest in us as individuals."

❏ "Stops, smiles, and says hello."

❏ "Knows every person's name and something about them."

❏ "Enjoys relationships with people who are not management and calls them by name."

Leaders who ignore the "softer side" of the job are sometimes described as "arrogant" or "prickly" or as needing "a refresher course in people skills." The real damage, however, can be seen in comments such as "I am uncomfortable around you," "I don't think we connect very well," or "he constantly has his guard up, so I can never tell what he's after." These kinds of feelings likely will not translate into enthusiasm for work.

In surveys, more than half of 2197 people could not give their bosses the highest rating on being easy to talk to. And 76 percent of 1783 people said that their leaders were not entirely "authentic." To be thought of as "real" and approachable, leaders must find their own style to make sincere connections. Some leaders have regular brown-bag luncheons with small groups. Others schedule weekly "walk-throughs" of the company, connecting with handshakes, quick conversations, or even just a wave and eye contact. A man I know who has had a very successful political career used to ask his three kids anytime they met someone: "What color eyes did he or she have?" He wanted to make certain that they were sharply focused on an individual in social interactions, not looking past the person or darting their eyes toward the ground or sky. Even more than remembering a person's name after walking away, he wanted his children to look a person straight in the eyes and concentrate on them. He understood how really connecting—not just going through the motions and gestures of common courtesy—was crucial to establishing trust and rapport.

When her mother became sick with cancer, Lynne shared the information with two people—her boss and a direct report who had just gone through a similar experience with a family member. "Sharing my struggle with my mom's cancer with my direct report created a level of compassion between us, underscoring that while we were professionals who worked hard together, we were also people." At her mother's funeral, which was held in a different state, several hundred miles away, Lynne was surprised to look out in the church and see her boss in a pew. "I was so moved that he did that, and it really increased my respect for him," she said. "He cared as much about me as a person as he did about me as a professional."

**In surveys, more than half of 2197 people could not give their bosses the highest rating on being easy to talk to. And 76 percent of 1783 people said that their leaders were not entirely "authentic."**

Review the following checklist to see whether you are giving people opportunities to really know you:

___ I make a point to know the names of people in my organization.

___ I am comfortable making small talk with people at all levels.

___ Developing strong relationships with my peers is a high priority.

___ I have a good balance between job tasks and building relationships.

___ I know the personal interests of my peers and direct reports.

___ I enjoy the opportunity to meet socially with peers and often do.

____I engage in casual conversation with people each day.

____I often stop to talk to my colleagues' administrative assis-
tants before a scheduled meeting.

____I usually know if something is troubling a person.

____I make sure my team has offsite meetings.

____My offsite meetings include social and recreational activ-
ities.

## LETTING YOUR GUARD DOWN

When a CEO recites the organization's values through a
microphone at a quarterly meeting, employees may think,
"We already know this. We've heard it before." The values
and the CEO are not connected, and consequently, the
employees likely feel disconnected, too. But when that CEO
personalizes the topic, perhaps by sharing how the values
have made a difference in his or her own work, the message
has more substance, more relevance, and more meaning.

Do you express what is important to you and why? Do
you invest time in personal conversations, making connections with your followers and letting them see the real you?
In order for leadership transparency to lead to credibility, you
must allow followers to see your humanness, too.

When followers understand a little about who leaders are
as people—their perspectives, their lessons, their personal
values—and the followers see a congruence between the
inner and outer person, they are more likely to trust those
leaders.

# CHAPTER 6

# Promises Made, Promises Broken

*Future leaders will be less concerned with saying what they will deliver and more concerned with delivering what they have said they would.*

—Dave Ulrich, NAMED BY *BUSINESSWEEK* AS ONE OF THE WORLD'S TOP 10 EDUCATORS IN MANAGEMENT AND THE TOP EDUCATOR IN HUMAN RESOURCES*

On the first day the country's major airlines began operating flights again after the September 11, 2001 terrorist attacks, Kathleen Holmgren was scheduled to fly from California to the Midwest. As senior vice president of Santa Clara, California–based Sun Microsystem's Network Storage Marketing Group, Holmgren was committed to leading a quarterly meeting in Colorado with approximately 100 Sun employees who were based there. But she, like so many Americans, was afraid to fly. "I was really scared about it, and my three children were saying, 'Mommy, please don't go,'" she said. After Holmgren and her husband discussed how best to handle the situation, she flew out as scheduled. She opened the meeting in Colorado by saying to the group of employees: "I felt like I made a promise to you so that's why

*The Leader of the Future, Jossey-Bass, San Francisco, 1996, pp. 212–213.

I'm here. But I also need to keep a promise to my family. I can't stay the four days that I said I would because my family is nervous about my being away from them." As for the rest of the nation, it had been an unsettling time for Sun employees. One of the company's directors was killed in one of the airplanes that crashed, and Sun also had had offices in one of the Twin Towers, although all those employees made it out safely, according to Holmgren. The Colorado executives were impressed with Holmgren's commitment to keeping her promise, and many of them thanked her during the question-and-answer portion of the meeting.

Maintaining our commitments and keeping our promises are difficult tasks in both our personal and professional lives, and the complex situations in which we find ourselves do not always provide a clear choice between breaking a promise and keeping it. Sometimes, in fact, the best choice is *breaking a promise as little as possible*.

For example, say that you have committed to attend a very important annual planning meeting concerning product development. The meeting involves members from three departments—engineering, sales, and marketing—and as head of marketing, you are expected to present valuable information on your company's competitors. Leaving the driveway on the morning of the meeting, two kids at the bus stop run toward your car and tell you a man in a truck twice drove slowly by the bus stop and looked "creepy." As someone who is part of the neighborhood watch program, you feel obligated to wait with these children and then report their concerns to the school's principal. You know that by doing so, you will be late for your important meeting—breaking your promise. However, your obligation to help, a promise you made when you became a part of the watch program, overrides the commitment you made to be at the meeting. To minimize the damage (to break the promise as little as possible), you call your assistant and ask her to pass the word that you will be late and that if you totally miss the meeting, you will provide your complete research in a written report by the end of the day.

You might think that the decision to fulfill your watch program duties is so clearly the right decision that there will be no negative consequences. After all, you are choosing children's safety over business. Your coworkers will not only understand your choice, but they also likely will admire it, too, right? This answer is not so clear. For example, if you are a person who frequently breaks promises (even for the right reasons), your integrity may be in question. People may start to wonder about all your "excuses."

It's a hefty word, *promise,* and it conjures up the big ones in life—marriage, an oath of office, a legal vow to "tell the whole truth so help you God." But credible leaders take everyday promises seriously, too. If we were to place the kinds of promises we make on a continuum, with absolute promises on one side (marriage vows, for example) and relative or "casual" promises on the other (such as saying to someone, "I'll call you right back"), the promise you made to be at that meeting would fall somewhere in the middle of the continuum.

←————————————————————————————→

**RELATIVE PROMISES**                    **ABSOLUTE PROMISES**

The consequences of breaking promises—including lost credibility—are likely to be far more serious on the absolute side of the continuum than on the relative side. How much your credibility is affected when you break a promise depends on both the level of the promise you made and how frequently you fail to fulfill your promises.

Whether you should or should not break an absolute promise is a complicated personal decision that does not belong in this book. Instead, we will examine the more relative promises, the ones people make—and break—in business everyday, the ones that affect people's credibility most often. Commitments to call someone, to honor a deadline, and to attend a meeting are all relative promises. Avoiding them is nearly impossible, and breaking them, unfortunately, is the norm. We easily slip into the verbal blind spot of overpromising. "I'll have the report to you by Tuesday" translates to "You won't mind if it's not to you until midmorning Wednesday, right?" "Let's do lunch" means "See you soon." "I'll call you" really means "I'll be thinking of you." Just because you omit the words *I promise* does not mean that you are held to a lower standard of commitment. Children sometimes will say, "Well, but I didn't *promise*" when they do not do what they said they would, but in grown-up reality, there is no such thing as "crossed fingers" to cancel out a commitment we chose to make.

Leaders who break commitments send loud messages through their organizations. According to a recent survey of 2700 CEOs conducted by management consulting firm Proudfoot, company chiefs arrive late for 6 in 10 meetings (*USA Today*, November 26, 2002). Chronic tardiness is a promise-breaking habit that sends a host of negative messages: "This meeting isn't really important." "A good work ethic—what's the big deal?" "I'm the big guy. I can do what I want."

Other promises are promises of confidentiality and *value promises*—commitments implied through the values we proclaim. These are often implied promises because the promise is never spoken but is instead understood without saying. An example of a value promise is a leader who begins a new campaign within his or her company for "innovation and creativity." If, within 3 months after the campaign begins, this leader rejects all suggestions for a new way of doing performance reviews and proceeds with the way they have always been done, then the leader's actions do not back up the values asserted with his or her words. In the eyes of the employees, this leader is breaking a promise.

When employees detect an inconsistency in a leader's words and deeds, trust decreases and morale turns sour. Before long, productivity—and the company's bottom line—is negatively affected. A study conducted by Tony Simons, associate professor of management and organization behavior at Cornell University, confirms promise-keeping's value to a company's bottom line. Simons' study involved 6500 employees from 76 companies in the hospitality industry, specifically hotels, but his findings certainly could apply to other industries as well. He found that an increase in score of only 1/8 point on a 5-point scale in a hotel's "behavioral integrity" (consistency between words and actions) on employee surveys would improve the hotel's annual profits by 2.5 percent of revenues. For an average full-service hotel, this is $261,000 added to the bottom line.

"Hotels where employees strongly believed their managers followed through on promises and demonstrated the values they preached were substantially more profitable than those whose managers scored average or lower," Simons wrote in the *Harvard Business Review* (September 2002). "No other single aspect of manager behavior that we measured had as large an impact on profits."

Yet even with promise-keeping's bottom-line benefits, research confirms that it is an unusual act in the workplace. In a study involving 700 people, a significant proportion of them chose not to keep their word even when told that breaking a particular promise had legal repercussions. The results showed that promise-keeping is a "very low priority in the workplace, a phantom work ethic rather than a core value" ("Promise-Keeping: A Low Priority in a Hierarchy of Workplace Values," by Ellwood F. Oakley and Patricia Lynch, *Journal of Business Ethics* 27: 377–392, 2000).

Our own research confirms that of 12,000 employees, 55 percent believed that a boss or coworker could improve in consistently keeping promises. And of more than 1100 leaders, 67 percent admit they have room for improvement in promise-keeping. Do you have room for improvement? Are you not keeping commitments and damaging your credibility?

> Of 12,000 employees, 55 percent believed that a boss or coworker could improve in consistently keeping promises. And of more than 1100 leaders, 67 percent admit they have room for improvement in promise-keeping.

# ARE YOU A PROMISE-KEEPER?

Using the following scale, rate each expectation of credible leaders in two ways:

How well do you think you are doing at meeting the expectation?

What might others think about how well you are meeting the expectation?

**SCALE:** 1 = significant improvement needed; 2 = slight improvement needed; 3 = skilled/competent; 4 = talented; 5 = outstanding: a role model

| EXPECTATION | HOW DO YOU THINK YOU ARE DOING? | WHAT MIGHT OTHERS THINK? |
|---|---|---|
| Displays willingness to say "no" to maintain business focus. | 1 2 3 4 5 | 1 2 3 4 5 |
| Makes realistic commitments (avoids overcommitting). | 1 2 3 4 5 | 1 2 3 4 5 |
| Always does what he or she says he or she will do. | 1 2 3 4 5 | 1 2 3 4 5 |
| Does not make unrealistic commitments for other individuals or his or her team. | 1 2 3 4 5 | 1 2 3 4 5 |
| Only cancels/reschedules appointments when critical. | 1 2 3 4 5 | 1 2 3 4 5 |
| Honors confidential information. | 1 2 3 4 5 | 1 2 3 4 5 |
| Avoids promises that are mere intentions (differentiates when he or she will "try" versus when he or she will "do"). | 1 2 3 4 5 | 1 2 3 4 5 |
| Is reliable and dependable. | 1 2 3 4 5 | 1 2 3 4 5 |

**MY SCORES:**

*Scoring yourself:* Add your total for each column. A single column score of 36 to 40 suggests that you are doing an exceptional job and are meeting others' expectations of someone who is a promise-keeper. A column score of 30 to 35 indicates that you have some areas for improvement; on issues as important as these, I believe leaders should strive to be "outstanding: a role model." Below 30 indicates a danger area, and you may be chipping away at your credibility. A discrepancy of more than 9 points between the two column totals indicates a possible gap in perception worth investigating. If your "How do you think you are doing?" score is higher than your "What might others think?" score, your intentions may be better than your actions. If your "What might others think?" score is higher, you may not be giving yourself enough credit for a job well done.

People who do what they say that they will do are rarities. These are people who are building reputations of credibility and trusting, effective relationships with their peers and followers, who will in turn go the extra mile for their leaders.

## MINDING OUR WORDS

Keith is an exemplary leader who inspires others with his vision for elder care. The growth and success of assisted living residences and services in his state were legendary, and when he announced his retirement after 20 years as chief executive officer (CEO), employees wept openly. Yet tears were shed not for their beloved CEO's departure but for Allen, the talented and experienced vice president of patient services, who was promised the CEO job and did not get it. Some said that it was an unspoken promise through the years, whereas others claimed that it was in writing, but the organization as a whole understood that Keith had been grooming Allen to be his successor. After behind-the-scene meetings with the board of directors, a new CEO was proclaimed—a capable vice president from another part of the organization who had been around for a couple of years.

In my coaching session with the new CEO, we talked about his challenges. "What's the fallout of this situation for you?" I asked. He said that he thought people fell into three different groups. For one group, Allen not getting the job was a blip on the radar screen, and they did not care much. Another group cared but would quickly move on. The third group concerned him. "They care deeply about Allen and the promise that wasn't kept," he said. "I don't know how deeply."

Thus, because of a broken promise—or at least the perception of one—a popular CEO retires with a stain on his credibility, an organization is fractured, and a new leader must take office in a sludge of left-over feelings. Some suspected that Keith did not keep his promise by fighting hard enough for Allen when the board began looking at other possibilities for a successor. It is also possible that Keith did all he could, but the decision ultimately was out of his control. And therein lies a problem with many promise-makers— committing to something without fully considering the variables and contingencies that may, in the end, despite all efforts, make keeping the commitment impossible. If Keith did indeed give impressions that his position eventually would be Allen's, he made a promise that was not his alone to make or keep.

The other lesson from this incident is this: Be careful what you *appear* to promise. Whether it is a real or perceived promise that is broken, the negative effects likely will be the same. In the workplace, those effects could be lost trust and effectiveness and decreased morale and productivity.

Leaders determined to be perceived as promise-keepers must seriously consider the growth goals they promise to employees, customers, and shareholders. This was almost surely the thinking behind Coca-Cola's December 2002 announcement that it would no longer play the earnings estimates game and would stop providing specific estimates on future profits. Assigning hard numbers to earnings predictions not only makes public a promise that possibly could fall flat, but it also places tremendous pressure on a company's internal structure to meet the performance expectations at any cost. While few companies will cut such large ethical corners as committing accounting manipulations or outright fraud to meet these public goals, many do fall prey to day-to-day leadership dilemmas of choosing the right way or the expedient way. Coca-Cola's decision to focus more on long-term performance measures in its investor education is likely to be followed by other companies.

While a culture of hype still exists in our country, recent corporate scandals have made underselling and underpromising a more prudent way to win loyalty. This is true not only for business leaders in their dealings with customers and investors but also for employees. Misrepresenting your company's culture and growth expectations in order to successfully recruit a top-notch sales rep, while tempting, can be expensive in the long run. An employee who is told about and understands the risks that come with a job is more likely to work through hard times or difficult situations. Likewise, being forthcoming with employees about what can go wrong in each step of a new business strategy builds far more stability than grand promises that may not be kept.

## KEEPING RELATIVE PROMISES

Nancy, a senior executive at a utilities company, was given high marks in an assessment survey by her eight direct reports on integrity, job knowledge, risk taking, and coaching—pretty important stuff. Her lower marks were in her consistency, particularly with returning phone calls.

"I never ever call unless it's important, but I can't count on her to get back real fast," one sales representative said. Another said: "I like the autonomy I get with her being my manager. On the other hand, sometimes I need her. And when

I do, she's slow about getting back to me. I never know how long it's going to be."

Like so many who do not keep relative promises, Nancy never intended to be unreliable. "I really mean to support my folks, but I get caught up in other things." We can all identify with this answer, but Nancy's good intentions do not go very far, and her lack of dependability is in direct conflict with her regular preaching about teamwork.

Of more than 1200 people surveyed in developmental assessments, 77 percent said that their leaders could improve at making realistic commitments. Those in leadership positions who cannot uphold their commitments risk not only their personal reputation but also their organization's reputation and morale. In our fast-moving and chaotic business environment, I am always amazed when I hear comments like these about people I coach:

❏ "I always know I will get an immediate response when I ask Sue for help."

❏ "Katy consistently follows through on everything that is promised."

❏ "David makes and keeps all his promises."

❏ "Joe does what he says he will do."

Why am I amazed? First, because such praises are rare. Second, because Sue, Katy, David, and Joe, just like you and me, are speeding through crazy days, and they actually can do these things!

**Of more than 1200 people surveyed in developmental assessments, 77 percent said that their leaders could improve at making realistic commitments.**

Many of us are guilty of overpromising and underdelivering. We commit to lunches, phone calls, volunteer events, speaking at the quarterly business breakfast, and so on, even when a voice in our heads is telling us not to. Why do we set ourselves up for such no-win situations?

Here are some reasons:

- ❏ We want people to like us, so we try to please them by saying "yes."

- ❏ We think that being a team player means we should never say "no."

- ❏ Saying "no" might make us appear uninterested and even selfish.

- ❏ We are not really sure that it will fit in our schedule, but we will go ahead and commit and can always cancel later.

- ❏ We are careless in making promises and do not first consider whether we are really capable of keeping them.

- ❏ We confuse being busy with being productive, so lots of unscheduled time on our calendars looks suspicious.

- ❏ We think we *should* be able to do all these things.

- ❏ Even though our words communicate a higher level of commitment, we are really thinking "I'll *try* to be there."

This last reason is brought up a lot in my seminars. Participants often complain of peers who say "I'll call and we'll do lunch" and are never heard from. They don't say "I'll try to call," so expectations are created. Good intentions perhaps, but unkept promises like these breed bad reputations and resentment.

Follow-through on commitments is not an easy feat. It takes organization, care, and attention to keep your reputation from falling in the "undependable" and "unreliable" categories. When you say that you are going to have your part of the report done, review the year-end goals over the weekend, schedule time to debrief an employee's presentation, stop by a colleague's office, or finish that overdue performance review, you are making a commitment. That the commitment may seem to you like a small thing in the midst of bigger ones does not matter. What is important is that another person understood that you said you were going to do something, and your failure to follow through will disappoint others and hurt your credibility.

There must be a great correlation between your words and your actions or you will be perceived as unreliable and lacking in credibility. Being known as a dependable person, a person who keeps his or her promises, sometimes only requires a higher level of organization (keeping a better calendar). More often, however, it requires that you better monitor what you say. After-the-fact excuses usually do not mean much. It also requires adhering to the following guidelines:

*Aim for clear communication to reduce false expectations.* Sometimes people are perceived as being unreliable because they are careless with their words. Statements that are meant as "good intentions" can be misleading because listeners often take them to be promises. Strive for clear communication at all times. And don't forget to first ask yourself: Am I going to *try* to do it, or am I going *to do* it? Do I mean to, intend to, or hope to? Or am I going *to do* it?

*Don't make unrealistic commitments for others.* Those who overcommit and underperform often damage not only their own credibility but also the credibility of the department, company, or organization they represent.

Donna is a bright, talented human resources (HR) manager who is very customer-focused. However, her team told me that sometimes her passion for pleasing the customer is damaging. She frequently overcommits, and things do not get done on time, they said. Donna overpromises, and the department cannot deliver. Consequently, her credibility—and her department's credibility—takes a beating. In a London-based marketing firm, Simone is "one of the smartest people around," but she often falls into the same trap as Donna. Said one of her peers: "She sometimes takes on more responsibility than she and her department are able to handle, which leads to extreme effort and still missed deadlines. Our reputation within the company is not good because of this." Larry, a successful entrepreneur and owner of a manufacturing company, gets so excited about his new products that he sometimes promises a delivery date that cannot be met. His missed delivery dates have become such an expectation that even the sales representatives who carry his line will not start selling the new product until they actually know it is in stock.

Before making a commitment, consider what other parties are accountable to your promise.

## All in Favor Say "No"

One of the best and most powerful words in building your credibility is *no*. "*No*, I can't do that this week." "*No*, I can't have it for you." "*No*, I'm not going to be able to change that." The person you say "no" to may not like it. He or she may be annoyed, frustrated, disappointed, or even angry. Credibility, however, is *not* a popularity contest. Saying "no" is much less damaging than generating mistrust.

When I moved my home from Atlanta to Pensacola, Florida, the moving company told me that my furniture would arrive on a Tuesday. On Wednesday, they said it would arrive Thursday, and on Thursday, I was told it would arrive on Friday. My belongings were finally in my possession on Saturday. When I complained to the highest manager I was allowed to speak with, he told me that the furniture was always scheduled to arrive on Saturday. Apparently my customer service representative knew all along that my possessions would arrive 4 days late but was trying to keep me satisfied. Obviously, while I would have been annoyed to hear on Tuesday that the furniture would not show until Saturday, I would have preferred an initial disappointment over a string of them. And the company, in my estimation, would have kept its credibility. Like most customers met with a broken promise, I would sooner move myself next time than use that company, and I go out of my way to tell others.

To avoid overpromising by saying "no," follow these guidelines:

1. *Do not stray too far from the path.* It is easy to spend time and energy on tasks that do not get us any closer to our ultimate desires. What is most important to you? What do you want to accomplish? Determine goals that reflect your core priorities, and do not allow yourself to be easily led astray. For example, if one of your core priorities is to spend more time coaching your direct reports, then spending a certain amount of time each week with them is an important goal. When non-goal-related opportunities arise, you may need to decline.

2. *Explain to ease the pain.* When saying "no" to someone, follow with a phrase of explanation—not an apology or excuse—to soften the blow. "No, I won't be able to make the benefit dinner. That's a really tough week for me at work." Let your priorities be known, and people likely will understand.

## Rethink Before Rescheduling

It happens all the time. You have to cancel the phone call, meeting, lunch—whatever. Maybe it is because you are truly overscheduled, overcommitted, and behind. Or maybe someone else has inconvenienced you. Don't think people notice when you cancel and keep rescheduling? Think again.

Andy is an HR professional who is fast gaining a reputation you and I do not want. One of his colleagues said, "I have observed, on many occasions, when Andy was committed to either attend an important meeting or facilitate a meeting elsewhere, that these commitments were canceled or postponed at the last minute. Others are concluding that Andy cannot be depended on and that he is not consistent. These last-minute cancellations seem to create a great impact on others in the department, and my sense is that our team and perhaps even people outside our team are losing respect for him. If there is some reason he can't attend these kinds of commitments, he shouldn't commit to them in the first place."

No one's calendar can or should be set in stone; flexibility is certainly important. But keep a realistic calendar, and avoid cancellations and reschedules. Otherwise, you risk appearing unreliable.

## HONORING CONFIDENTIALITY

Donald, a senior executive in the western division of a national nonprofit organization, said that he would "walk through walls" for his boss if it weren't for one thing—his boss can't keep a secret. Donald had spent 16 months wooing a highly prized individual, Wade, from the California State Department and had designed a reorganization to leverage Wade's significant relationships within the state in hopes of bolstering the nonprofit's donations. People in the State Department were not going to be happy about losing Wade, and Donald committed to keeping the information confidential until an appropriate time. Donald reminded his boss about the importance of keeping everything under cover until all details were cemented.

Several weeks later, at a conference, Donald was having a conversation with another employee from the State Department who casually said, "I hear Wade is leaving us." Donald swears that there was a twinkle in the man's eye. If word had gotten out, Donald was certain the source of the leak was his boss, so he spoke with him again about the importance of keeping the information confidential. Again, a few weeks after the conversation, at another conference, a State Department employee crossed the room and said to Donald, "Hey, I heard Wade's leaving us to join you."

In both situations, Donald was forced to be as vague as possible in order to honor the confidentiality agreement. Donald resented his boss for not respecting the commitment and felt that by not doing so, he was putting both Wade's and Donald's reputations in question. "He gets caught up in the glory of the moment, and he can't contain himself," Donald said. "Recruiting Wade was a huge coup, and my boss almost ruined it."

As the cornerstone of many professions, such as doctors and lawyers, violating a code of confidentiality not only ruins a reputation but also could have serious legal repercussions. As an executive coach, my ability to maintain confidentiality is directly related to my success. I could have the best coaching skills in the country, but if I blab when I promised not to, I will lose business. Confidentiality is so important to people—especially in a business setting—that even *appearing* to not maintain it to the highest level can make others uncomfortable and put your integrity in question.

Mike Silvers, a branch manager for Disney's Vista Federal Credit Union, which serves 60,000 members, used to answer calls to his cell phone while surrounded by employees in the lobby of his branch. Then he learned in a performance survey that his commitment to honor confidential information was in question.

"Many of the calls I receive are about sensitive issues, and when I'd answer these calls in the lobby, people became concerned that I wasn't honoring confidentiality to the highest level," Silvers said. "It didn't happen often but enough to bother staff." On receiving his employees' feedback though a 360-degree assessment, Silvers immediately worked to correct the misperception by walking to a private area or to his office when he received a call on his cell phone.

When someone asks, "Can we keep this confidential?" they are asking you to "cross your heart and hope to die" that you will not utter a word about what is told. Do not take this promise lightly. A breach in confidentiality wipes out trust and can destroy a relationship. And recognize that expectations of confidentiality are sometimes unspoken. When someone shares personal or sensitive information with you, they might not say, "Please don't tell anyone," but it is likely their unsaid wish and expectation. Their willingness to share such information indicates they trust that you will respect their privacy and to not do so will seriously diminish the relationship.

Not honoring that trust is an unabashed broken promise that others may never overcome.

Although all personal and sensitive information probably should be treated as confidential, if you are still in doubt, ask. It is better to get clarification with the person who shared the information with you than to take liberties and make assumptions.

## VALUE PROMISES

John is a charismatic owner of a $40 million manufacturing company with 75 employees. Revenues are up 20 percent, and the future looks bright. John eats and breathes customer partnerships. "Focus on the customer," is his mantra. In his private life, John has a penchant for expensive sports cars, and he owns a 75-foot yacht. At work, his salespeople are begging for better cell phone coverage and personal technology to keep in touch with customers while on the road, and employees in shipping want a new computer program so that they can access the shipping software and better serve customers.

"We don't get it," a sales rep said. "We're working our butts off, and this company is very successful. He says, 'Focus on the customer,' but when we ask for a cell phone that works in Alabama, he says, 'No.'"

John's messages appear mixed, and mixed messages confuse people and damage credibility.

A leader's promises are constantly under scrutiny, particularly during times of organizational difficulty or change, such as layoffs, reorganizations, or stressful business conditions. When a leader backs off from a promise during these times, he or she plants seeds of suspicion and distrust. Yet followers expect leaders to make and keep value promises. Leaders are always under pressure to make promises, and value promises—commitments in word and behavior to particular ideals—are inherent in true leadership.

As a leader, what kinds of value promises do you make?

❑ The promise that your followers can entrust their future to you

❑ The promise that those who follow you can achieve their potential

❑ The promise that you are prepared to lead

❑ The promise that you will practice what you preach

A leader should not say that quality is important and then not give people the resources to improve quality. He or she cannot lecture about teamwork yet support structures that encourage individual achievement or turf building. And when a leader who wants to appear progressive espouses "empowering people" but still micromanages, the results are sour.

Value promises are often broken because leaders have personal priorities or styles that conflict with the organizational values or because they have unclear priorities. Managers who are unsure of their personal priorities or their organization's priorities will be more likely to change management approaches after reading the latest business book or magazine article. Management styles can be trendy. Ten years ago, creating a "learning organization" and "reengineering" were popular. Now, General Electric's quality program "Six Sigma" and the innovation process of IDEO, the world's largest design firm, are popular and also may be abandoned in time. While employees usually appreciate leaders who attempt to stay on top of the latest management research and who are willing to try new strategies, they may be cynical of leaders who shift from one fad to another too often.

As a leader, be careful of the explicit and implicit promises you make to your followers, and keep the following in mind:

❑ *Like it or not, you are highly visible.* If you are in a leadership position, always remember that you are under scrutiny. Take time to remind yourself of the promises you have made and to evaluate how your actions measure against your promises. Get a pulse on whether others feel that you are keeping your value promises by asking for feedback informally or through surveys.

❑ *They often hang on every word.* What growth goals have you revealed to your investors? What kinds of career growth or opportunities for your employees have you hinted are possible? *These may be seen as promises.*

❑ *Your philosophies could imply promises.* Are you someone who regularly repeats sayings that may indicate your beliefs or attitudes toward the way things should be done? "Attitude determines your altitude." "No question is a stupid question." "Hard work never goes unnoticed." Depending on the context of when you espouse these time-worn phrases, be aware that you may be implying a promise.

Dave Marnell, a small-business owner in Pensacola, Florida, had one of his value promises put to the test and, in the eyes of his employees, came out shining. He had long told employees at his dry cleaning company, "You're equally important as our best customer." One morning, while still at home, Marnell received a call from Martha, an early-fifties worker at his Diamond Cleaners. Through tears, she recounted an irate phone call she had just received from a customer complaining about a botched order. Diamond's home delivery man had only dropped off half the customer's order, overlooking another order due to the home; it was a simple mistake that could be corrected by redelivery. The customer issued his complaint through "screaming" and various profanities, which made Martha shake and cry. She explained to Marnell how the order got messed up, and they determined a solution.

But Marnell also was concerned about how Martha had been subjected to such abusive behavior from this customer. Later, after arriving at the store, he again went over the incident with Martha. Then, with Martha at his side, Marnell called the customer and apologized for the mistake in handling his cleaning order. But he did not stop there.

"What you did to my staff member was totally out of line. No one should have to put up with that. We have your clothes, but before you get them, I'd like for you to give a sincere apology to Martha."

The customer responded with more profanity and hung up. Ten minutes later, he called back and told Marnell that he had had a bad day and was sorry for his behavior.

"Sir, you are apologizing to the wrong person," Marnell said.

The following day, the customer came in with a formal apology for Martha, who had been told by Marnell that if she did not think the apology was sincere enough, she could reject it and not release the rest of the customer's order.

"Without my staff, I couldn't put out the product that attracts my customers," Marnell said. "It takes a good year to really train a staff member, and losing one can be detrimental to the big picture."

Some business leaders, taking the attitude of "the customer is always right," would never have done what Marnell did. Leaving aside the debate over which customer service approach has more merit, the point is this: Marnell made a promise, and he kept it. He said that his employees were equally as important as his customers, and his actions backed up that value.

## DOING WHAT YOU SAY YOU'LL DO

Promise-keeping in leadership is not always clear-cut. Sometimes leaders are forced to reconsider promises and disappoint followers. Those are the times when transparency is particularly important, because followers who understand the reasoning behind broken promises may be more accepting of the consequences.

The personal reward for keeping promises and fulfilling commitments is a reputation of reliability and of meeting a key expectation of credibility. It is a worthy goal. Start really listening to yourself when you are interacting with others. Are you speaking or implying promises that you may not keep? Do your actions match your words?

Globalization, virtual teams, workplace diversity, de-layering, information technologies, and complex alliances assume new associations and networks of trusting relationships that hinge on a consistent congruency between words and actions. Trusting teams or organizations start with leaders who demonstrate congruency between what they say and what they do. When managers match their words and actions and others follow their lead, reliability and dependability infuse daily dealings with suppliers, customers, and business partners. These are big bottom-line payoffs for leaders who keep their word.

........................................................................

# CHAPTER 7

# Deliver Bad News, and Do It Well

*It's no use saying*
*"We are doing our best."*
*You have got to succeed in*
*doing what is necessary.*

—Winston Churchill

W hen Hyperion Solutions, a $500 million performance management software company, faced a merger gone sour and a slowing economy, the chief executive officer (CEO) hired Amelia Tess Thornton to help pull the company through. As chief administrative officer (CAO), Tess Thornton was asked to help take $69 million off the bottom line and find a way for the Sunnyvale, California–based company to remain profitable at a time when most software companies were not. When it became clear that 10 percent of the publicly held company's 2500 employees would have to go, Tess Thornton immediately turned to the challenge of how best to handle the layoffs.

"There was tremendous pressure to keep things quiet," she recalled. "Layoffs were happening all over the [Silicon] Valley, and the common approach seemed to be to terminate employees on a Friday afternoon so you could ship them out as quietly as possible and hope that the employees who remained would somehow forget about the losses by Monday."

Hyperion chose a different route. First, it announced almost eight weeks in advance to its employees that layoffs were imminent. Even though specific information—which positions or departments would be affected—was not yet known or could not yet be divulged because of Securities and Exchange Commission requirements, Hyperion leaders tried to be as open as possible. "It was extremely difficult," Tess Thornton told me. "People were afraid at first."

By being candid from the beginning, Hyperion was able to get valuable input from second- and third-level managers, who were asked to participate in the process of determining where the cuts would occur. The managers also were given training in how to handle employees during difficult times and how to deliver bad news, because it would be they—not the head of human resources (HR) or other senior management—who eventually would inform individual subordinates that they had been laid off. "Employees want to hear that kind of news directly from their supervisor," Tess Thornton said. "Plus we wanted to give the people who were remaining a chance to show respect to those who were leaving and, in a way, be able to grieve the loss." Up to the actual layoffs, Hyperion tried to quell rumors by allowing employees to ask any question and setting up a blind mailbox on the employee Web site for those who felt more comfortable asking questions anonymously.

Also, instead of the touted strategy of choosing Friday afternoon as the time to communicate the bad news, Hyperion leaders chose Tuesday morning. "While Friday certainly would have been easier for us, it would have been the worst thing for those remaining because they would have been left to worry all weekend," Tess Thornton said. "By choosing Tuesday, we had the whole week to talk with employees, meet with them, and correct any misperceptions. Consequently, by the weekend, people felt better."

While the managers who personally handled the layoffs felt the weight of such a difficult task, several later described the event as one of the proudest moments in their careers. According to Tess Thornton, "They told me they believed they honored the people who left, that they had been given enough information and felt prepared to deliver the message."

By focusing on communicating tough information in ways that showed respect, integrity, and care, instead of taking shortcuts for expediency's sake, Hyperion ultimately benefited through increased, long-lasting morale. Said Tess Thornton, "It totally changed the trust level that the employees had in senior management."

Delivering bad news can be tricky business, yet doing it well is an essential part of leadership transparency that builds credibility and is a leader's opportunity to visibly demonstrate his or her commitment to honesty. We all have been on the receiving end of bad news, and we know how it feels. When it is not delivered well, we can feel a sense of betrayal, anger, and indignation. Trust is destroyed, and relationships suffer.

For most people, delivering bad news is hard. Some leaders opt for silence, and whether their intentions are good or not, that is probably irresponsible. Those on the receiving end usually appreciate bad news that is delivered promptly with honesty, directness, care, and concern.

## STAND AND DELIVER

Delivering bad news does not have to be demoralizing or damaging to morale or relationships. Doing it well probably requires forethought and planning, however. It is important to know your purpose and expectations before you inform the troops of disappointing or potentially controversial news. In approaching each situation, ask yourself

❏ What is my purpose?

❏ What outcome am I hoping for?

❏ What are my concerns?

People will have a range of emotions that you have to anticipate. What might their reactions be? What questions could they ask? Prepare yourself by putting yourself in their shoes.

When you are ready to deliver, make sure that you do it in person whenever possible, and keep these guidelines in mind:

*Offer as much information as you can.* Some people believe that "less is better," but this approach can backfire. Employees may feel as if they are not able to be trusted with all the information or that they do not deserve to have it. Lack of information also can cause the remaining employees to fear the unknown, thereby affecting the quality of their work and the quality of their lives.

*Allow for questions.* Not giving people a chance to ask questions sends a terrible message. You should have already anticipated what they might ask, and you should be prepared and willing to answer any question as openly as possible.

*Deliver as soon as you can.* Do not get too hung up on choosing the right timing for delivering bad news because waiting and delaying can be inconsiderate and disrespectful and could cause the recipient to feel that you are being less than forthcoming. The best time for bad news is usually now.

During a major reorganization, Anne, a plant manager for a large telecommunications company, had to face her five direct reports with information regarding their termination or reassignment packages. Anne had already received her package; she was headed to South America to a larger plant and was looking forward to the experience. However, while she also knew what was in store for her team, she had not told them. It was December 14, and Anne did not want to tell two of them that they were being terminated. She also did not want to tell the other three that they would have to move their families if they wanted to stay with the company.

Several members of her team had already been to her and said, "Anne, we know you know, so why don't you just tell us?" She had been evasive, and said, "Look guys, it's almost Christmas. Just go home, enjoy the holidays, and we'll deal with the packages when we get back."

After 11 months of working hard to build credibility with her team, Anne was getting ready to make a major mistake. I coached Anne and told her that she needed to deliver the bad news immediately. The next day, she told me, "I did what you told me to do. I called everybody in this afternoon, sat down with each of them, and told them about their terminations or relocations. It was tough. I was trying to sugarcoat it a little bit by waiting and letting everybody enjoy their holidays first. But that was my agenda, not the right agenda." Anne also believed that her team appreciated her being candid as soon as she could, and several thanked her for doing what they recognized was difficult but allowed them to spend their holidays without the burden of uncertainty.

## HANDLING PERFORMANCE ISSUES

Mike Harreld, CFO of Georgia Power Company, a subsidiary of energy company Southern Company, has a kind of personal litmus test for whether he may have performance issues to deal with among his team. "When I get a call from my boss telling me about a particular problem that needs to be solved, I try to pay close attention to my gut after I hang up the phone with him," Harreld explains. "During the first 30 seconds after a call like that, I consider who I want in my office to help me resolve the problem and why. More importantly, I consider who I don't want in here and why. Chances are, those are the weak links I need to deal with."

Many leaders, even when they are aware of the weak links, are slow to address them because doing so probably involves uncomfortable conversations.

Surveys tell us that leaders do not always step forward and communicate directly. Of 1784 employees who participated in leadership assessments, 75 percent said that their bosses do not always deal with issues in a candid manner, and 72 percent of those leaders' peers agreed. Employees

Of 1784 employees who participated in leadership assessments, 75 percent said that their bosses do not always deal with issues in a candid manner, and 72 percent of those leaders' peers agreed.

often beg for more constructive criticism: "Give me clear feedback more often, even when it may be difficult for me to hear." "Tell me where I stand. Tell me what I'm doing wrong." If you have ideas and information that will help someone perform better, your responsibility as a leader is to share that information. Helping your followers succeed is part of your job.

## HOW GOOD ARE YOU AT DELIVERING BAD NEWS?

Using the following scale, rate each expectation of credible leaders in two ways:

How well do you think you are doing at meeting the expectation?

What might others think about how well you are meeting the expectation?

**SCALE**: 1 = significant improvement needed; 2 = slight improvement needed; 3 = skilled/competent; 4 = talented; 5 = outstanding: a role model

| EXPECTATION | HOW DO YOU THINK YOU ARE DOING? | WHAT MIGHT OTHERS THINK? |
|---|---|---|
| Effectively deals with individuals whose behavior undermines teamwork or partnerships. | 1 2 3 4 5 | 1 2 3 4 5 |
| Effectively works through conflicts to create positive solutions. | 1 2 3 4 5 | 1 2 3 4 5 |

| | | |
|---|---|---|
| Confronts and deals with integrity problems (regardless of personal risk). | 1 2 3 4 5 | 1 2 3 4 5 |
| Provides constructive feedback that is specific, timely, behavioral, and balanced. | 1 2 3 4 5 | 1 2 3 4 5 |
| Is clear and upfront with bad news (no hidden agendas). | 1 2 3 4 5 | 1 2 3 4 5 |
| Creates a safe environment for sharing bad news. | 1 2 3 4 5 | 1 2 3 4 5 |
| Encourages others to share bad news (does not shoot the messenger). | 1 2 3 4 5 | 1 2 3 4 5 |

**MY SCORES:**

*Scoring yourself:* Add your total for each column. A single column score of 31 to 35 suggests that you are doing an exceptional job and meeting others' expectations of someone who knows how to deliver bad news well. A column score of 26 to 30 indicates that you have some areas for improvement; on issues important as these, I believe leaders should strive to be "outstanding: a role model." Below 26 indicates a danger area, and you may be chipping away at your credibility. A discrepancy of more than 8 points between the two column totals indicates a possible gap in perception worth investigating. If your "How do you think you are doing?" score is higher than your "What might others think?" score, your intentions may be better than your actions. If your "What might others think?" score is higher, you may not be giving yourself enough credit for a job well done.

When leaders do not deliver tough information such as constructive performance feedback, they are often holding back for reasons that are unsound.

## ELEVEN THINGS WE TELL OURSELVES
## TO AVOID GIVING BAD NEWS

1. *I don't think she can handle it.* If you deliver the message in a respectful and constructive way, most people can take it and indeed often appreciate it.

2. *I'll hurt his feelings.* You might, true. This is often what makes delivering bad news hard to do, especially if you truly care about the other person. Ultimately, however, how are you hurting the person if you do not give him or her the information?

3. *She will get emotional.* If your listener tears up or gets angry, you will live through it. Be empathetic, and keep the conversation moving and on track—the other person usually will follow.

4. *He will get defensive.* Not everyone is good at receiving tough information, and defensiveness is a natural tendency, particularly if your delivery is harsh or otherwise uncaring. If the defensiveness gets unproductive, point it out, and get to the source of it before moving on.

5. *I am sure that she already knows.* People tend to assume that other reasonable people will see situations as they see them. Yet one of effective communication's most important bylaws is: Never assume anything. Even if the person really is all-knowing, hearing the issue from you likely will add another perspective that might make a meaningful difference.

6. *He should already know.* Now you have coupled the breaking of "never assume anything" with a bad attitude. Whether you believe the person should be able to intuit your perception of a performance issue is not the point. As a leader, you have a responsibility to communicate.

7. *She will think that I am singling her out.* She also may feel particularly valued because her boss cares enough to tell her what is getting in the way of her success.

8. *It is only my opinion.* If you are a well-regarded leader, your followers probably value your opinion.

9. *He will think that I do not like him.* This likely will not occur if you position your constructive criticism around specific behaviors—not the person.

10. *It will ruin our relationship.* When bad news is handled well, it usually changes relationships for the better.

11. *The situation may take care of itself.* Most situations do not solve themselves magically, so holding onto this rationalization serves only to help you delay something that is difficult and uncomfortable but probably necessary.

When I began coaching executives, I used to dread sessions that required me to deliver difficult news: "Others find you obnoxious and unfair." "You take all the glory." "Sleeping with the boss is hurting your professional image." I was particularly uncomfortable when the person I was going to sit down with had already established himself or herself as being closed to feedback or defensive or as having a temper problem. "Gee, this is going to be fun." Experience taught me that my internal self-talk was unreliable. Even when those on the receiving end were defensive, hurt, or indignant initially, they usually realized that I was there to help. The messages often resulted in breakthroughs; a situation was clarified, perceptions changed, and a greater understanding—both of themselves and of others—emerged. And knowing that I had helped someone usually brought a sense of great satisfaction to me.

How do people like their bad news? Usually straight up and right across the table. A leader who does not sugarcoat but instead delivers difficult information in an honest, direct, and caring manner shows responsible transparency and builds credibility. And followers are more likely to accept and act on constructive criticism that is developed and communicated fairly and respectfully. Communicate the bad news eyeball to eyeball, and follow these guidelines:

*Imagine your boss.* No matter who you are talking to, pretend that you are giving the bad news to your boss. Use the same tone, body language, and words that you would with your own manager to maintain a respectful approach.

*Be careful of the easing-in method.* When we have to communicate disturbing information, we often look for ways to make the job easier. One technique people learned years ago was to sandwich bad news in between good stuff. *Tell them two good things, and then throw in the bad news.* People on the receiving end of this approach usually see it coming. And while they are anticipating your actual point—the bad news—your lead-ins of positive information may seem insincere and merely charitable. A balance of positive and negative feedback is only necessary over time—not during one meeting. If you still feel that it is beneficial to include positive feedback in with the bad news, then consider ending on the positive note instead of easing in with it.

*Do not hint around.* An indirect strategy whereby you make up your mind about an issue and then try to get the employee to see it your way by asking carefully designed questions reflects a narrow mind. Don't ask, "Have you ever thought of signing up for a presentation skills course?" if you really mean, "You're going to need to make better presentations if you want to continue moving up in this company." Also, don't start your conversation with questions like "Are you aware that we have a problem?" or "Do you know why I've called you in here?" Making people play guessing games is insulting and likely will send their minds reeling in a hundred different directions, conjuring things they "might've done" and diffusing the import of the real point you are about to make.

*Concentrate on behaviors.* Discuss the performance issue, not the person. For example, "Your monthly status reports aren't thorough enough," not "You are careless and lazy." Also, it is not your place to overanalyze another's mind-set, uncover deep-seated reasons for his or her behavior, or solve personal problems. Leave that to psychothera-pists, counselors, and ministers.

*Allow the person to respond.* You may have made a hasty con-clusion that the person's performance problem was due to his or her disposition instead of specific work-related circumstances. Allow the person to clarify and explain matters. He or she may have an alternative explanation that you were not aware of that may sincerely change how you feel.

*Do not allow the discussion to stray.* Keep the communication moving and on target. You may need to say, "That's important, but it doesn't have anything to do with why we're here" or "Good point. We may need to talk about that at a different time." Determine the amount of time you think will be necessary to have the conversation, and stick to it. Keep working toward the desired conclusion.

*Do not get stuck in the past.* It is possible for a difficult conver-sation to stay in the past where the performance problem occurred. Do not allow the issue to be described, explained, and dissected over and over again. Move to the future, because that is where the necessary action is required for improvement.

*Determine a plan.* How is the problem going to be resolved? Or how will the employee improve? At first, see if the other person can design his or her own plan of action. You likely will get more buy-in and better results that way. You can help him or her along by offering your opinions: "Here's what I see. . . ." "I think if I were you. . . ." "These are the options from my point of view. . . ."

Sometimes performance issues are more complicated than helping good employees get better. Employees with negative attitudes, slackers, or otherwise bad team members can erode workplace morale and rob organizations of synergy. They drive high achievers, competent employees, and hard workers wild. When leaders do not handle these situations promptly, failing to hold everyone accountable, a team's valuable members can lose faith and become cynical and frustrated, and the problem can escalate. One employee said of her boss: "By the time he deals with it, it's a whole lot bigger than it would have been." Failing to handle and adequately document poor performance also can result in potential legal problems for the organization.

Yet managers often put off squarely dealing with underperformers, and many are aware of their tendencies to do so. In surveys, 91 percent of almost 1000 leaders said that they need to improve in effectively handling team members whose behavior undermines teamwork or partnerships. Of 8229 of those leaders' peers and direct reports, 79 percent agreed that there is work to be done.

> **In surveys, 91 percent of almost 1000 leaders said that they need to improve in effectively handling team members whose behavior undermines teamwork or partnerships. Of 8229 of those leaders' peers and direct reports, 79 percent agreed that there is work to be done.**

When a leader's followers know that he or she is aware of an underperformer or problem employee (maybe they have even told him or her) and the leader fails to do anything, the followers shake their heads in disbelief. Do not alienate your prized team members. Swift action creates a culture that says nobody gets away with anything. People like and respect that.

When a team member is undermining your group in some way, follow these guidelines:

1. *Do not assume that peer pressure will take care of it.* Some people never respond to peer pressure. Besides, the peers have work to do, and dealing with Alan's bad attitude is not their job—it is yours.

2. *Setting high expectations does not prevent problems.* It is not good enough just to communicate expectations. The second half of the performance equation is measuring against them. "This is what I expect. This is what you're delivering." Correct mismatches immediately.

3. *Always follow up.* The problem may not be solved with one conversation. Meet once a week for a month and review how things are progressing. If things are not improving, you will need to consider alternatives.

4. *When appropriate, tell people what you have done.* If the problem was a blatant or ongoing one and the team suffered, communicate that you are on top of it. You do not have to give the details, but reassure them that you are taking charge.

## DELIVERING BAD NEWS TO YOUR BOSS

When Carolyn, a vice president of marketing at a large design firm, and her assistant could not find the files for a project they had been working on, their search revealed that Carolyn's boss, without communicating his plans, had given the project to a newly hired vice president. "Can you imagine? He takes the project away and didn't even come to talk to me. I could have spit I was so angry," she recalled. Carolyn was admittedly delighted when the new vice president, 6 months after being hired, was terminated because he did not "fit the culture."

"Did you get the project back?" I asked.

"Are you kidding? Giving it back to me would have been an admission of his poor hiring decision," Carolyn said.

I asked her why she had never told him about how upset she was over the situation, especially when it first happened.

"Oh, he knew," she said. "He had to know."

People who do not communicate with their leaders about unpleasant or disappointing issues are only hurting themselves. Even the best of leaders have blind spots, and an overlooked problem or a misaligned strategy should not be assumed to be intentional disrespect or harm. Leaders manage huge workloads and aggressive deadlines and simply may fail to consider a possible outcome. While many organizations have formal methods such as anonymous surveys to help leaders know where things stand and how they are performing, these methods are not usually enough. Your leader may need to hear some bad news in between formal assessments.

This checklist is a good place to begin thinking about how good you are at sharing tough information with your leader:

____ I disagree with my boss when I feel strongly about something.

____ I see it as part of my responsibility to give my boss an alternative point of view.

____ I am smart enough to know when to disagree with my boss and when not to.

____ I would never challenge my boss in front of his or her peers.

____ I weigh the risks against the benefits before giving feedback.

If you have decided to have that tough conversation with your boss—the one about how he or she is undermining you in your relationships with customers or how you believe that the marketing strategy for next year fails to tap a key customer base—think carefully. Ask yourself, What is my desired outcome? What are the possible negative consequences? Will someone else be affected by my decision to go forward? What will happen if I do not speak up? After you are clear about your purpose, possible risks and repercussions, and the outcome you are hoping for, plan your part of the discussion. In telling your boss bad news, you will need to

*Present a solid case.* Do not just go in with personal opinions. Present the facts, including real numbers or evidence or specific examples of the behavior you are addressing. Do not exaggerate, and make sure that you use neutral language. For example, "You say things that make me feel insignificant, particularly when we are around customers" is much better than "You treat me like a child."

*Offer a fix.* You do not want to just be a complainer. If appropriate, propose a workable solution. For instance, if you are pointing out that his or her marketing plan ignores a key customer base, then present an alternative that stays within budget.

## PUTTING THE WELCOME MAT OUT FOR BAD NEWS

Leaders who do more than claim an "open-door policy" will be more likely to have bad news—potentially valuable information—brought directly to them instead of having to dig for it or, worse, learning about it too late. If you are surrounded by people who cannot or will not tell you the hard truth, check yourself. Are you making it clear that you expect bad news to be communicated? Are you creating a safe zone for it?

Mike Harreld, the previously mentioned Southern Company executive, has learned that as leaders are promoted higher and higher within an organization, the harder it becomes for them to get people to bring them bad news. "Most want to make you feel good and kiss up," Harreld said. After 20 years with Southern Company Services and now one of its top leaders, Harreld says that he looks for people he can depend on to give him the tough information, and he "picks at them." He asks them questions: "Anything I need to know about?" "What do you think about this?" "How do you think this is going?" "And then you shut up and listen," Harreld said, adding that leaders should never, never shoot the messenger and never react defensively. "It took me years to learn how not to [be defensive]," he said. "But I had to learn, because I need information from people."

To ensure that you remain fully informed about problems that may affect your success or issues that require resolution, create a transparent culture within your team or organization that makes delivering bad news simply part of doing business. Consider these strategies:

*Make it part of the drill.* As part of every new strategy, policy, or analysis, designate a "devil's advocate" or a worst-case-scenario team. This helps make bad news legitimate and even sought after.

*Do not respond to "kissing up" behavior.* If you visibly reward people when they tell you what they think you want to hear instead of what you want to know, you devalue bad news.

*Ban PowerPoint.* Or at least do away with canned presentations at internal meetings that are meant to keep employees informed of the company's progress. You do not want to give the impression that real information is being "prettied up," filtered, or massaged.

*Reward it.* When people bring you bad news, thank them for doing so, and recognize their courage. If the news made a difference in some way, let people know.

*Now do something.* You have been told the bad and the ugly. So now what? If you make a habit of not responding to bad news that is delivered to your doorstep—even only by acknowledgment—people eventually will not see the use.

## BEING TRANSPARENT IN TOUGH SITUATIONS

Being forthcoming with bad news—whether controversial information about policy changes or reorganization or constructive criticism that may be upsetting to an individual—and building a transparent culture that makes bad news safe are essential in earning and keeping a credible reputation. And being open to bad news can help an organization stay on track and use all its resources.

Are you sluggish in facing tough situations that require you to talk openly with your followers? Do you choose expediency over candid communication that honors your followers? Do you encourage others to bring you bad news?

During skittish economic times especially, leaders should not hide; they should be front and center, allaying fears by keeping the team well informed. With employee performance concerns, leaders are expected to act swiftly, helping their followers improve or dealing with weak links in the group. And always, credible leaders must deliver bad news with respect, dignity, and care.

# CHAPTER 8

# Get Ahead,
# Say You're Sorry

*If we are lucky, what will come of this
sorry mess is a wider awareness that
virtue is rooted in surely acknowledging
where we have gone wrong.*

—Ellis Cose,
"LESSONS OF THE TRENT LOTT MESS,"
*NEWSWEEK*, DECEMBER 23, 2002

Mike Ruettgers, executive chairman and former chief executive officer (CEO) of EMC Corp., a publicly held technology company, has been successful in part because he has learned how to clean up some serious messes. When he joined EMC in 1988, the company's data storage products were failing at a rate of almost 50 percent, a crisis that was pushing EMC toward bankruptcy. In an attempt to contain the damage to the company's reputation and credibility, Ruettgers tirelessly traveled the country to meet with customers, apologizing for the problems associated with EMC's products and promising to make things right.

The meetings were extremely difficult for Ruettgers, then executive vice president of operations and customer service. He experienced first-hand the far-reaching effects of EMC's product failures and played the humiliating role of the company punching bag. One customer, Ruettgers recalled, broke down in tears. "He started crying and said, 'If you don't get this fixed, I'm going to get fired.'"

After patiently listening to their complaints, Ruettgers offered customers a humble apology and a choice—a new EMC system or one made by competitor IBM but paid for by EMC. At the time, many of EMC's customers were small to medium-sized businesses that depended on EMC's products to run their operations. "We felt we had to offer replacement systems or these businesses may not have survived," Ruettgers told me. "Yet providing those substitute products was very expensive—it almost bankrupted us." Indeed, so many customers chose IBM storage systems that during several months of the following year, most of the boxes shipped by EMC contained its competitor's products.

Ruettgers' strategy allowed EMC to keep all but one customer, and today the company has a truly amazing reputation for customer service and boasts a customer retention rate of 99 percent. Its service unit uses a "guilty until proven innocent" approach to all its customer inquiries, tackling system problems that ultimately may prove to originate with a competitor's piece of equipment (about 20 percent do). Much of EMC's reputation and tremendous growth—annual revenues were $123 million in 1988 and grew to $7.1 billion in 2001—are due to the leadership of Ruettgers, who during his tenure was named one of the "World's Top 25 Executives" by *BusinessWeek*, and the belief that how you handle mistakes actually may be more important than getting things right the first time.

In a world where perfection, confidence, and winning are pervasive values in work and life, it seems ironic that there could be success in admitting mistakes and saying that you are sorry. In fact, admissions of failures and, if appropriate, genuine apologies offered and accepted can be very powerful. Even with its inherent risks—such as appearing weak, incompetent, or otherwise less than perfect—confessing mistakes signals courage, accountability, and humility. Indeed, mistakes are an opportunity to visibly demonstrate a commitment to honesty. And handling mistakes with a high degree of responsible transparency helps to build a leader's reputation of credibility.

When details behind the Enron scandal began to trickle out and the finger pointing began, it became evident that many involved knew of foul play long before the company's collapse. Until the subpoenas began to arrive, Enron managers and executives at Andersen, the accounting company that enabled Enron's bad moves, kept their heads down. No one yearns to blow the whistle on his or her company's wrongdoings—too many risks and repercussions, like making enemies or losing a job. But we are not talking about serious white-collar crime here. If you are part of Enron-type illegalities, you are definitely not practicing transparency, and credibility is the least of your worries. With more honest mistakes, the everyday human errors we can all make in business, how well we handle them can seriously affect our credibility. Airing mistakes and apologizing require great care and excellent judgment in order to minimize possible risks and repercussions, such as a dip in others' loyalty, trust, and confidence or the loss of a customer, friend, or job, depending on the level of the crime.

*Not* airing mistakes can be just as risky, though. These days, it is almost impossible to keep your bad moves a secret because too many opinionated and well-informed people have access to e-mail and the Web or they are onto you via plain old good intuition. After the recent string of corporate scandals, if you do not lay all your cards on the table and look failures in the eye, people just may assume that you are a cheat. Indeed, this is part of the reasoning behind the wave of companies that now strive to appear transparent.

This chapter offers suggestions aimed at helping you to handle your mistakes well so that you can strengthen your relationships and your credibility. Do you handle mistakes in ways that build credibility? Or do you choose behaviors that might chip away at your hard-earned reputation for credibility? Assess your performance with this quiz.

## HOW WELL DO YOU HANDLE MISTAKES?

Using the following scale, rate each expectation of credible leaders in two ways:

How well do you think you are doing at meeting the expectation?

What might others think about how well you are meeting the expectation?

**SCALE**: 1 = significant improvement needed; 2 = slight improvement needed; 3 = skilled/competent; 4 = talented; 5 = outstanding: a role model

| EXPECTATION | HOW DO YOU THINK YOU ARE DOING? | WHAT MIGHT OTHERS THINK? |
| --- | --- | --- |
| Willingly admits his or her mistakes. | 1 2 3 4 5 | 1 2 3 4 5 |
| Treats mistakes as opportunities for learning and positive change. | 1 2 3 4 5 | 1 2 3 4 5 |
| Effectively apologizes in a timely and sincere manner. | 1 2 3 4 5 | 1 2 3 4 5 |
| Forgives others' mistakes and does not hold a grudge. | 1 2 3 4 5 | 1 2 3 4 5 |
| Avoids blaming others. | 1 2 3 4 5 | 1 2 3 4 5 |

**MY SCORES:**

*Scoring yourself:* Add your total for each column. A single column score of 22 to 25 suggests that you are doing an exceptional job and meeting others' expectations of someone who willingly and effectively admits mistakes. A column score of 19 to 21 indicates that you have some areas for improvement; on issues as important as these, I believe leaders should strive to be "outstanding: a role model." Below 19 indicates a danger area, and you may be chipping away at your credibility. A discrepancy of more than 6 points between the two column totals indicates a possible gap in perception worth investigating. If your "How do you think you are doing?" score is higher than your "What might others think?" score, your intentions may be better than your actions. If your "What might others think?" score is higher, you may not be giving yourself enough credit for a job well done.

## WILLINGNESS IS KEY

In one of the biggest art scandals in recent history, Sotheby's former chairman, A. Alfred Taubman, went so far as to depict himself as "dumb" and "hungry" in order to seem unaware of his company's illegal collusion with competing auction house Christie's. Long thought of as archrivals, the two auction houses were exposed by a 4-year investigation of price fixing, cheating their customers out of more than $400 million. Both houses admitted to the conspiracy—and paid $512 million for the misdeed—but Taubman, who was found guilty in December 2001, tried to get out of a prison sentence by presenting himself as unaware of his company's wrongdoings and as an elderly man (he was 76 at the time) inclined to catnaps and more interested in lunch than in Sotheby's bottom line.

It is astonishing what people will do to protect their reputations. Owning up to a misdeed is often a last-resort measure. Former U.S. Senate Majority Leader Trent Lott made a bigger mess for himself when he did not immediately recant and apologize for his remark that if America had elected Strom Thurmond during the 1948 presidential election, when he ran as a segregationist protest candidate, "we wouldn't be in the mess we are today." Lott's first attempt to dodge a controversy began "with the classic words of the non-apologetic apologist, expressing sorrow if anyone had taken offense at his remarks, and making an oblique reference to 'discarded policies'" ["Fire Trent Lott" (editorial), *New York Times*, December 12, 2002, p. A34]. As everyone, including some of Lott's Republican peers, continued to express outrage over his comments, Lott's explanations got increasingly humble in tone until he eventually said what sounded like a true apology and regret over his words at Thurmond's birthday celebration. Whether a more forthcoming apology would have allowed Lott to remain as majority leader is doubtful, but he surely would have quelled the media frenzy and public backlash had he been willing to immediately offer up humble apologies.

It is unlikely that our mistakes will make the news or be contemplated behind bars. Instead of suffering newsworthy public humiliation, we often can make amends for our wrongdoings by presenting ourselves to those we have harmed, choosing the right words in offering our regret, and hoping for forgiveness. And yet, in business, we usually do not. Admissions of mistakes do not flow easily in the workplace. In assessment surveys, 62 percent of leaders said that they could improve at admitting mistakes.

> **In assessment surveys, 62 percent of leaders said that they could improve at admitting mistakes.**

I once coached a driven, successful senior executive of a major financial company on developing his leadership skills. While we were reviewing feedback from his direct reports, John, in his middle fifties, began pacing back and forth in his Manhattan office. He could not understand why all eight of his direct reports scored him low on their expectation that he "willingly admits mistakes," whereas he had rated himself as high as possible.

"Obviously," he reasoned, "they read the question wrong or didn't understand it." I expressed doubt and noted that they seemed to read and understand correctly the other 68 questions. John received high marks on a number of other behaviors of credibility. This one was apparently not his strength.

"But Barbara," he pleaded, "I do admit my mistakes."

Trying to make sense of the situation, I sat quietly for a minute, and then I asked, "John, do you *willingly* admit your mistakes?"

He didn't hesitate. "Hell no, not *willingly*. But I do admit them."

There's a big difference between *choosing* to confess and *having* to confess. The people who worked for John were not misreading that question on the assessment surveys. They fully understood it and made a valuable observation about one of John's behaviors that was damaging his credibility. Willingness is key. Being sincere and forthcoming in admitting your mistakes is far more meaningful than having them dragged out of you.

Clearly, there's much to consider before rushing forth with your wrongdoings. There are risks, the severity of which is usually tied to the consequences of your mistake and whether it was made honestly or deliberately. And the risks and repercussions often are not clear until after you have spilled the beans, making whether to do so in the first place a very difficult decision.

My colleague, Tom Heinselman, once coached a Fortune 100 company's female executive, Claudia, who received terrible ratings on integrity in a 360-degree assessment conducted with all seven of her direct reports. Claudia, it turned out, had created a mess for herself in trying to help her boss, who was competing for a new position with the head of another business unit within the company. To improve her boss's chance of winning the promotion, Claudia withheld business information from the other unit that could have helped its quarterly revenue picture. As a result, her unit looked better, and so did her boss. Claudia's team knew what she had done and told her through her 360-degree assessment that she was way off base. Tom suggested to Claudia that she get her team in a room, admit the wrong, apologize, and commit to making it right. Claudia expressed concern that the company's top management would find out about her wrongdoing and she might lose her job. Tom argued that she had essentially already lost her job because she could never be an effective leader with her current team unless she made amends. "I also told her she was in a fantasy if she thought her seven direct reports were the only people who would ever know about what she had done," Tom said.

Tom was right. In the long run Claudia would have been much better off accepting the risks of facing her team. She had made an error in judgment, and it was no secret. While stepping forward and showing accountability could have resulted in Claudia losing her job, she would have at least allowed herself the chance to earn back her reputation. By not handling the mistake properly, she reinforced her discredit and still remained vulnerable to be fired. (Tom never found out what Claudia chose or how things turned out.)

Tout the merits of admitting mistakes in certain work climates, and it sounds like a loud belly smacker hitting the water. Organizational experts tell us that teams and companies with low-trust environments—usually rooted in an organization's structure, processes, and practices—set the stage for hiding mistakes. If your boss owns the business and is a micromanager on the lookout for every little thing you do wrong, the notion of revealing errors could cause you severe lip quivers. In a work culture where a "rank and yank" philosophy rules, is it really smart to admit a mistake when your mistakes are being tallied? We all wrangle with how to clean up our messes. If your situation is complicated and you are unsure whether to confess, ask yourself these questions:

❑ Will this indiscretion keep me up at night?

❑ Will other people suffer because of my failure to come forward?

❑ If I explain my decision to a person who respects me, what might he or she say?

❑ What is the worst thing that can happen?

❑ If I do not confess and someone uncovers it, what might happen?

❑ Five years from now, will I be proud of this decision?

It is entirely possible that a mistake can cost you a job, but most of the time I do not find people dismissing a chance to demonstrate accountability because of some high-stakes consequence. Instead, they are not honest about their mistakes because doing so would be uncomfortable, unpleasant, and hard to do. People respect humility, and that is what is required in admitting fault. The leaders I coach often expect to be judged harshly for acknowledging weaknesses or offering apologies, yet they typically end up being trusted and respected more, not less.

And handling mistakes well, as EMC proved, can be a powerful, good business practice. Mike Woods, M.D., an expert in physician leadership, encourages his doctor clients to openly acknowledge minor errors because it can reduce the risk of punitive actions. According to a study conducted by California's Loma Linda University Medical Center, patients are significantly more likely to consider litigation if a physician fails to disclose moderate or severe mistakes. Woods adds that when doctors not only admit to severe mistakes but also apologize, the chance for a malpractice suit is lowered by 50 percent (author interview on 5/21/2003 with Mike Woods, M.D., founding director of the Woods Development Institute and author of "Applying Personal Leadership Principles to Health Care: The DEPO Principle," American College of Physician Executives Publication, Tampa, Florida, 2001). If you have made a mistake that has legal implications, get yourself a lawyer. Legal brawls aside, however, studies show that customers appreciate companies that show accountability.

According to one survey, companies can get as much as 50 percent of their former customers back simply by picking up the phone and apologizing for past mistakes (*Your Company* magazine). Often all it takes is a conversation in which a company representative apologizes for a past flub—a late shipment, a miskeyed order entry, and so on. The apology— which costs the company nothing—makes the customer feel valued, so he or she is more willing to return. Some companies know so well the power of apologies in sustaining a solid reputation that they offered "apology bonuses" to class of 2001 MBA students. After offering jobs to graduates, Cisco, Intel, Dell, Sapient, and Nortel, tightening their belts because of a slipping economy, had to rescind their offers. The bonuses were up to 3 months' salary.

We work fiercely to protect our reputation and appear competent, so it seems dangerous to point out our mistakes. Doing so would make us look weak and cause others to lose confidence, we think. Yes, it may—especially if done without thought and preparation. Done well, however, admissions of failures are a show of strength and credible transparency.

## EFFECTIVE CONFESSIONS

At a leadership seminar for a credit card company, I asked each participant to come to the session with an unresolved situation that he or she as a leader was wrestling with. David, a middle-forties vice president, explained that his problem was a guilty conscience. During a stressful moment in a heated discussion, David explained, he had lost his temper with a colleague at a team meeting. "It was 6 weeks ago, and now I'm waking up in the middle of the night thinking I owe him an apology. I made a mistake."

In small groups, each person was instructed to role-play how he or she would handle the problem and get feedback from the group. I got the video camera ready while David set up the scene with another participant who would play the role of the colleague who got lashed by David's anger. The role-play began. David revisited his haunting moment, but then he seemed to go on, and on, and on, explaining himself.

After 5 minutes I turned off the camera and stopped the role-play. "David, what are you doing?"

"I am trying to say, 'I'm sorry.'"

His colleagues answered before I could: "Then just say it!"

The role-playing began again, and David again recalled the meeting when he had lost his temper. Then he said the words he had struggled with—"I am sorry."

Afterwards David told us, "It was very hard to say those words." Apologizing, he explained, meant that he had to own the failure publicly, which seemed a worse situation than just moving on and not acknowledging the bad treatment. "But just because I didn't acknowledge it didn't mean I was fooling anyone. In fact, I've felt a coolness from him ever since that meeting," David said. "We both knew I was in the wrong, and I'm sure the other colleagues who were in that meeting felt the same way."

When an apology is due but not given, a crack surfaces in the foundation of the relationship. No matter how much time goes by, the crack likely will remain. The relationship may still function, but without a solid foundation, it will never reach its potential. A good apology repairs the crack and, hopefully, allows the relationship to return to what it was. Very often all a person needs is to hear a sincere "I'm sorry," and you are back in the gold. In some cases an apology even can make the relationship stronger.

Even a wrongdoing that you are certain will go unnoticed by everyone could weigh on your conscience, and carrying around the guilt could negatively affect your confidence and performance. By being open about the error, you ease yourself of some of the burden.

Think of how you feel when someone comes to you and admits a mistake and maybe even sincerely apologizes. You likely feel respect for that person and gratitude for his or her courage in coming forward. When and how you handle mistakes are crucial. Follow these guidelines:

*Move from defense to offense as quickly as possible.* People tend to blame everyone but themselves—it is a natural defense to protect our self-image. If your performance is at question or if someone is upset with you, do an honest self-evaluation. No one will believe that you are truly sorry or are moved to change if you cannot even admit to yourself that you played a role in your unfortunate circumstances. The sooner you move to addressing the problem, the better you will be in the long run.

*Validate the other person's feelings or complaint.* You may not agree that you were harsh with your employee, and you may think that his or her gripes are petty, but that is not *his* or *her* reality. Even if you do not believe that you were "wrong" in the true sense, realize that others have unique perspectives that you may need to accommodate—or at least accept—if you are to have a good relationship. If you have offended someone, even unintentionally, you will lose nothing by at least acknowledging the other person's hard feelings and noting the misunderstanding.

*If appropriate, apologize—and to the right audience.* Depending on your situation, an apology may be in order to show regret and to start the process of healing. For example, if you have wounded another's self-worth or if your mistake results in a colleague losing an account, saying you are sorry can heal bad feelings and help you to maintain self-respect.

*Do not make a blunder of your apology.* Realize that actually saying the words "I'm sorry" or "I apologize" is crucial if you really intend an apology. When President Clinton gave his televised address to the American people following the release of the Starr report, he never actually said, "I'm sorry." His choice of words did not go unnoticed. In fact, Clinton's obvious omission overshadowed everything else he said and was the topic of discussion in the coming days—until he finally said the words. By then, some people were unconvinced that Clinton's apology was sincere. The apology without the "I'm sorry" likely will not work. If you try to deliver an apology without saying "I'm sorry," you are missing the point. And the other person will miss the point, too. Also be careful with the word *but* when making an apology. "I'm sorry, but . . ." is almost always used to *justify* one's actions. It is placing blame on someone or something else. It is saying, "I only did this because you did that." The net effect is an apology that does not really sound like an apology, and—to the offended—it probably does not feel like one either. If you do choose to apologize, do not broadcast your "sorry" beyond those you have wounded and those who need to be reassured. You do not earn extra forgiveness and sympathy by involving peripheral parties. Also, it is important to hit a balance between admitting your mistake in a professional way and putting yourself down for making the mistake. Note the difference between saying, "I'm so, so sorry. It's all my fault" and "I take responsibility for what has happened, and I assure you that it will not happen again. I have learned some valuable lessons from this, and here is what I am going to do differently."

*Be timely.* If President Clinton had admitted an improper relationship right when Monica Lewinsky's name surfaced, he could have apologized and saved himself from such a damaging and humiliating scandal. Instead, his too-late "I'm sorry" was never enough. U.S. Representative Gary Condit faced a similar situation over his alleged relationship with Chandra Levy. After weeks of refusing to speak to the press, he broke his silence—although still refusing to answer many questions—in an interview with Connie Chung. Not soon enough, Americans said in a Gallup poll, which also confirmed that 66 percent believed that Condit was not justified in refusing to respond to Chung's questions about his relationship with Levy, that more than 7 in 10 people believed that he owed an apology to his constituents and the Levy family, and that an overwhelming majority said that he was "immoral," "dishonest," and "uncaring."

Frequently your wrongdoings are not the secrets you thought them to be, so your timing in admitting those mistakes and apologizing is important. Less significant wrongdoings such as arriving at a lunch meeting a few minutes late or taking too long to return a phone call can turn into personal offenses if apologies are not made promptly. Greater misconduct usually requires a more thoughtful reaction. Saying that you are sorry immediately after being dishonest or humiliating an employee in front of his or her peers probably will not sit well. You risk seeming insincere and even belittling. It may take days or even months before both parties understand what happened and how the relationship was affected. Taking time to carefully think about the event can dignify the apology and ensure forgiveness.

Making amends requires planning. You should take the time to think about what you will do to make sure that you do not make the same mistake twice and how you can patch up what has been destroyed.

*Show sincere empathy.* Show regret and empathy when appropriate. "I regret what I have done" and "I know that I have let you down" can be healing words. Groveling, however, is seldom necessary, so be dignified about it. Do not give people the impression that you are looking for reassurance.

Anne, a sales manager for a telecommunications company, used an anecdotal example in one of her team meetings that she meant as a positive illustration of turning an angry customer into a return buyer. The anecdote involved Dave, one of Anne's direct reports. Dave was upset about being exposed in front of his peers. While the story illustrated Dave's ability to act on his feet and turn a bad situation into a payoff, it also revealed how Dave upset the customer in the first place. Most of all, Dave was angry because Anne did not ask permission to tell the story. In Dave's mind, Anne had betrayed his trust.

Anne knew that she needed to apologize in order to rebuild Dave's confidence in her as a leader, but she felt that Dave's reaction was "a little silly" and oversensitive. She went through the steps of an effective apology, and her delivery was good but for one thing: "She didn't grovel enough," Dave said. "I'm not sure she really understands what upset me."

Ultimately, Anne's apology was not effective because Dave did not accept it. Anne went through the motions of an apology because she needed Dave to remain a loyal and motivated follower. She said all the right words, but she did not come across as sincere.

A true apology requires one to empathize with the wronged person—or at least to accept the complaint as valid, if only in his or her eyes. An effective apology is difficult. If your soul is not rumbling a bit, your heart probably is not in it, and sincerity will not be perceived. And an insincere apology may be worse than none at all. Apologies that are motivated by guilty fear, a desire to please, or grudging compliance are not worth much. An effective apology begins with a dose of shame. You admit that you made a mistake and that you are ashamed of your behavior. You should feel low.

*Speak plainly.* Do not try to whitewash or avoid clearly naming your crime. Doing so can give the impression that you do not feel truly accountable or that you do not fully appreciate the consequences of your actions.

Dan, an early-thirties account executive for a software developer, recalls a time when he received an ineffective apology. Acting as team leader for a particular project, Dan got an ugly reaction from a coworker when he checked on the coworker's progress. "Really, he was taking out on me the fact that he had other demands and wasn't completing his tasks on time. He was so nasty that I avoided him for a couple of days, mostly because I didn't want to be subjected to such an attitude again. When he finally acknowledged his behavior, he only described it as 'being a little too animated.'" Dan resented the choice of words. And the trust and respect that he once had for the coworker were depleted.

In another incident, Craig, chief financial officer for a cable company's western division, was forced into a very late night preparing his presentation for the second day of his monthly meeting with 17 team members because Craig's analyst, Allen, was 4 hours late in getting vital information to him. When Craig finally received the e-mail containing the attachment, he read Allen's brief comment: "Sorry this didn't get done on time." Allen's apology was not nearly good enough because he did not take ownership. He also said nothing that reassured Craig that it would not happen again.

Consider the words of former Senator Bob Packwood, who was accused of sexually harassing at least a dozen women during his tenure in Congress. His 1994 apology outfailed even former President Richard Nixon's Watergate pseudoapology: "I'm apologizing for the conduct that it was alleged that I did."

*Tell what you have learned.* The time you admit your mistakes can be a great time to show what you have learned. The lesson is likely to be just as valuable for your followers. And helping your people grow and develop, even through your own mistakes, is part of true leadership. Communicate your course for corrective action. Pay close attention to those involved, and even ask for feedback.

*Move on.* Once you have done all you can to make amends, let go. Be patient, and others likely will move on, too.

## OVERUSED AND UNDERVALUED

While most of us have a hard time admitting mistakes and apologizing, some people cannot stop saying that they are sorry. People with this tendency definitely risk appearing weak.

The problem often lies with the double meaning of *sorry*, and men and women tend to use the word differently. Saying "I'm sorry" can be meant as an apology, and this is usually how men use it and interpret it. However, these words also can be used to express regret ("I'm sorry that happened") or to show empathy ("I'm sorry that you're having to deal with this"), and women tend to imply these meanings with "I'm sorry" more than men.

Cheryl, a vice president of finance for a regional bank, had to report in a board meeting that revenues were down for the fiscal year's first quarter. At the end of her statement, she used the words "I'm sorry," and the CEO reacted by saying, "Well, you don't have to apologize, Cheryl." Cheryl only meant that she was disappointed that revenues were not stronger. Yet she appeared to the CEO to be making an admission of fault or unnecessarily taking responsibility for something that was not her responsibility at all. Unfortunately, the exchange occurred in front of other key executives of the company, making Cheryl look weak to a number of important people.

Gender differences aside, apologies are sometimes given unnecessarily: "Sorry you're having a bad day." "I'm sorry, you've reached a number that is no longer in service." "Sorry about the bad weather." When *sorry* is an easy and overused word, it loses value. And apologizing too often and for the wrong reasons seems self-deprecating. Of course, if you are really making that many mistakes, you should carefully evaluate your performance. Others certainly are.

Do you see yourself in these everyday situations?

1. When your boss cancels out on your quarterly meeting, do you express your disappointment to the team by saying that you are sorry?

2. The waiter brings you a lamb chop that is rare, and you ordered it medium. When you call him over, do you say, "I'm sorry" before asking him to take it back?

3. Have you ever apologized because it is raining?

4. When the dry cleaners failed to get the spot out of your tie, did you tell them that you were sorry you had to bring it back?

5. When your mail service does not pick up on time and the package will be a day late, are you sorry?

6. When your partner has to have a root canal and you feel bad for him or her, do you say that you are sorry?

7. Your new human resources director insulted a coworker in your meeting. Are you sorry you have to talk to him or her about that?

8. You start talking at the same time as another person. Are you "sorry"?

If you are a person who tends to overuse *sorry*, consider reserving it for times when you are actually apologizing and want to be taken seriously. Instead: "I feel badly about your root canal." "It's unfortunate that we have to talk about the insult you hurled at the sales director." "I regret that my mail service wasn't on time."

## TAKING RESPONSIBILITY

Leaders who want to be perceived as having credibility must master the art of handling mistakes properly. When—not if—leaders commit errors in judgment, unintentional offenses, or flat-out blunders, they then have a chance to practice responsible transparency and build respect.

Commander Scott Waddle was recently relieved of his command of the *U.S.S. Greeneville* after the nuclear attack submarine collided with a Japanese fishing boat, an accident that killed 9 people and injured 35. Waddle did not hesitate in taking responsibility and issued wrenching and raw apologies throughout the following months when he underwent public humiliation and recrimination. "My test has been, 'Am I willing to compromise my integrity?'" Waddle said in an interview with *Time* magazine. "I cannot tell you how easy it would have been for me to say it wasn't my fault—that the guys who worked for me made the mistakes. But I couldn't in good faith do that." Ten months after the accident, he returned to Japan to face the victims and the families of the 9 who died. Once again, Waddle apologized in tears (Jiji Press English News service, Tokyo, December 15, 2002). He lost almost everything, including his Naval career, but he is still considered credible and is admired by sailors around the world.

Have you done something that others might view as a personal offense, a broken confidence, a lack of support, an unkept promise, or as in Scott Waddle's case, an honest mistake? You now have an opportunity to visibly demonstrate your commitment to honesty and accountability. Admitting mistakes and apologizing demand strength and courage, and risks and repercussions are often inherent. However, taking responsibility for errors—not hiding from them—and making amends for any incurred losses or offenses are crucial elements of responsible transparency that help leaders and companies build credible reputations.

..................................................................

# CHAPTER 9

# Watch Your Mouth

*Any fool can criticize, condemn,*
*and complain—and most fools do.*

—Dale Carnegie

E d, the sales manager for Ridgewood Properties, a $30 million real estate company, cursed and yelled at Frances, a member of the company's cleaning staff, in front of prospective customers and current residents of an upscale retirement community. Apparently Frances had not cleaned one of the model homes quite to Ed's liking, or he was just having a bad day—no one ever really knew the reason for Ed's harsh words because it never mattered.

Russ Walden, retired chief executive officer (CEO) and former owner of Ridgewood Properties, had made it clear to his 200 employees that he believed in treating everyone with respect. Each member of the Ridgewood team was given a copy of "Russ Walden's List of Thoughts on the Management Process," an informal writing by Walden that made known his philosophies about how work should be played. The handout opened with "The personal dignity of each individual is inviolate. A manager who often breaks this rule will eventually self-destruct—but we will probably get him (or her) first." By "dressing her down" in front of others, Ed, who had already been counseled for publicly criticizing people, had violated Frances' personal dignity. Walden fired Ed the following morning. Ed could not believe that he was being fired for "cursing a cleaning girl."

Walden admits that the decision to let Ed go cost the company. It had happened at the beginning of the sales cycle, a critical time in the real estate business "when all the good sales managers were taken," so Ed would be hard to replace. In addition, Ed's wife, a sales manager at another Ridgewood property, promptly left (as Walden knew she would) when Ed was terminated. Ridgewood was out two key people at a critical time. "It's hard to say how much, but I know we lost money from that situation," Walden told me. "But you have to do what's right."

In the long run, however, Walden's reputation for showing people respect turned out to be a winning business strategy. A few months later Walden paid a visit to the new sales manager hired to replace Ed's wife. While the manager gave a tour to an elderly couple considering a move to the Ridgewood retirement community, Walden chatted with their son, who said that he and his parents had narrowed their decision down to two retirement homes—both Ridgewood properties. The man's mother really liked the property they were currently looking at, but, he said, she felt badly that the sales manager at the other Ridgewood property had spent a lot of time with them and would lose the sale. Walden told the man not to worry about it, that Ridgewood had a fair compensation plan for its employees. "We look after our people," he said.

The son replied, "I already know that" and proceeded to tell Walden how he had heard from a friend the story about Ed getting fired. "I decided then that Ridgewood was for us," he said. "I figured a company that cared that much for a cleaning lady would probably care a lot about my parents."

Destructive comments come in many forms, including blame, gossip, criticism, sarcasm, inappropriate humor, and "us-versus-them" attitudes. They can pervade an organization and create a cynical, unsupportive culture. And these days, destructive comments abound. Disgruntled workers are whining regularly in Internet chat rooms and flocking to Web sites that cater to unhappy and angry employees.

Leadership that builds and maintains credibility requires transparent communication that shows the highest respect for people. Language that divides or is otherwise destructive can undermine the whole reasoning behind leadership transparency—to improve relationships, increase trust, and build a credible reputation. And leaders who avoid destructive comments have a much better chance at improving morale, strengthening teamwork, facilitating open communication, reducing turnover and absenteeism, and improving productivity.

## LANGUAGE THAT DIVIDES

Marshall Goldsmith, named by the *Wall Street Journal* as one of the nation's top 10 consultants in executive development, defines a *destructive comment* as one that does not add value and does not help you or others get the job done.

Such statements are hardly thought about and often just roll right off our tongues. The negative effect is very subtle and can go unnoticed by those making the remark. Some of these comments are clearly hurtful, others are wrapped in nuances, and others make us smile and laugh. But most destroy trust and chip away at credibility.

> In developmental assessments, 88 percent of leaders admitted that they could improve in avoiding destructive comments, and 83 percent of their bosses agreed.

Are our leaders watching their mouths? Not nearly enough. In developmental assessments, 88 percent of leaders admitted that they could improve in avoiding destructive comments, and 83 percent of their bosses agreed.

Destructive comments sound like

❏ "Paul's got a good heart. It's just that his people skills suck."

❏ "Do I want to go to Arnold's team meeting? Sure, I like watching incompetence at work."

❏ "Do you remember how we said there could never be anyone as bad as Helen? Think again, our new boss is a piece of work, believe me."

❏ "Of course, Sue is the queen of smarts. And her ego won't let us forget it."

These comments are not beneficial in any way. Some may be an attempt to point out an underlying issue or conflict that needs to be resolved. For instance, perhaps Arnold has a performance problem or Sue's know-it-all attitude is negatively affecting team members. However, there are more effective ways to bring about solutions.

Because destructive comments are often funny and said without thinking, avoiding them requires discipline and restraint. You must think before you speak, making sure that your comments about another person offer value of some kind or at least are neutral.

I once coached a young executive, Joan, who was very witty and smart. On a survey of credible behaviors, her team of coworkers scored her a low 1.5 out of 5 on "avoids destructive comments." Yet Joan's direct reports—not her peers—scored her very high. They did not hear destructive comments from her.

"I know enough not to do this with my direct reports," she told me. "But whoa, when I get in the conference room with colleagues and shut the door, we do let it all hang out! And I thought it was okay to do it there."

But it wasn't okay, and her credibility with her colleagues was suffering for it. Although other team members saw the fun in it—and even joined in—Joan's credibility rating was taking a hit.

Research seems to confirm that, like Joan, leaders tend to watch their mouths in front of direct reports but suffer from loose lips when they get around their peers. In developmental surveys, 75 percent of leaders' peers said that improvement was in order in avoiding and discouraging destructive comments about other people and organizations, whereas only 58 percent of the same leaders' direct reports agreed.

Another top-notch manager I coached had one of the sharpest wits I have encountered. A good sense of humor can be a great addition to a leader's toolbox if it is exercised with caution. This particular leader had not mastered avoiding destructive comments while being funny. And, oh boy, was he funny; I had to hold my side as he would go from one zing to another. But just because his comments were hilarious did not mean that they were appropriate in an organizational setting. After discussing with him the possible pitfalls of these funny one-liners, he said, "Well, I'll just have to cut down."

> In developmental surveys, 75 percent of leaders' peers said that improvement was in order in avoiding and discouraging destructive comments about other people and organizations, whereas only 58 percent of the same leaders' direct reports agreed.

"Do you want to be funny or credible?" I asked him. Reducing the number of destructive comments you make will not necessarily improve others' perceptions. People do not say, "Oh, he used to belittle me all the time, but now he only does it five or six times a week. Isn't that great?" If you are serious about improving your credibility, you will avoid the habit of making destructive comments as much as humanly possible.

## TALKING DOWN

When John Heer, president of Baptist Hospital in Pensacola, Florida, and senior vice president of Baptist Health Care, eats lunch in the company cafeteria with his frontline staff, they like it. One staff member says that it makes her feel "very important." While John's staff appreciates his giving them an opportunity to have conversations—whether they are about

serious business concerns or casual revelations about life outside the office—they also value the *way* that he talks to them.
"He talks to us in a down-to-earth, regular guy sort of way,"
one told me. This comment says a lot about John, especially
considering the great divide in professional status between
John's position and his frontline staff's.

Another leader I coached was not perceived as well as
John. At the pharmaceutical company where he worked,
Todd's direct reports and peers felt that he conveyed a "better than" attitude. With a doctorate in clinical psychology and
a rich vocabulary, Todd may have intimidated some—even
unintentionally. When you have become a leader because of
what you are capable of and what you know, it is tempting to
see yourself as better than others. But I do not believe that
Todd was actually arrogant. He was in fact a very fun and caring person, and I liked him a lot. In sessions with his direct
reports, I learned that they felt that he talked too much, and
a few did not like his use of "big words." I suggested to Todd
that he sometimes check with his people to see whether they
want the 5- or 10-minute version of an explanation or discussion. "I have used this technique before, and it's a good one,"
he said. "People always want the short answer." He was correct; people generally do want the shorter version. The point
of Todd asking the question, however, is to help people
understand that he is working on this issue and to help him
remember to be aware of how long he talks. Ultimately, Todd
has to learn to monitor his airtime and be conscious of how
his listeners perceive him.

Addressing the issue of Todd's rich vocabulary was not so
clear-cut. Someone who happens to have an admirable command of the English language certainly should be able to enjoy
using it. On the other hand, smart leaders work hard to break
down barriers within their organizations, and words sometimes create barriers. One of Todd's colleagues suggested that
he avoid his "high-level vocabulary" when talking with certain groups so as not to be seen as "talking above."

Getting at the root of perceived arrogance is sometimes difficult. People can be arrogant in very subtle ways. A parental tone of voice, a slight cock of the head, or a condescending look—any of these combined with a tendency to talk a lot or listen less can give others a bad impression. Learning about that bad impression through 360-degree performance surveys can be brutal, especially when you are actually meek in spirit. There is often an uncomfortable silence in a coaching session when I ask, "What are you doing to create this perception of arrogance?" Sometimes I already know the answer because the person is talking down to me; this turns out to be a good situation because I can call it to the person's attention and even mirror it for him or her on the spot. Other times the executive is not sure what he or she is doing, and we have to dig for the answers.

Ask yourself:

❏ *In my interactions with other people in my organization, who does most of the talking?* If others rarely take an opportunity to speak, consider whether you are hogging the airtime or, worse, acting in a way that makes them feel they should not speak.

❏ *Do I overlook people who might offer meaningful ideas?* If you really believe that others' opinions and input are valuable, then show it. Ask for their thoughts, and really listen to their replies.

❏ *When I offer advice, was I first asked for it?* This is not to say that you should only offer advice when asked; after all, one of a leader's responsibilities is to develop his or her followers, and that is a difficult task if the leader has to wait for prompting. However, some people like to hear themselves talk. Make sure that you are not one of them.

❏ *Do I know when to stop?* When talking to others, watch how you are being received. Learn to intuit when enough is enough.

## UNBRIDLED CRITICISM

Once, after helping a retail company develop a customized survey to assess its executives' performance, I attended the company's meeting for its top leadership, where the head of human resources (HR) presented the new survey, its purpose, and its process to all the managers. During the break, I was approached by Sue, the director of learning, who also had played a key role in developing the survey. "Did you notice the way my boss introduced this new survey like she did most of the work? She didn't do anything much except look over the work that you and I did. You know that." Actually, I had noticed that she had taken most of the credit, but when acting as a consultant, I usually do not expect any recognition—so it had not bothered me. Sue went on: "She does that all the time—takes the credit. If she ever asks me for feedback, I'll tell her, too."

While Sue may have had a valid point, her criticism was inappropriate and damaging to her credibility because by telling me—a third party—she appeared untrustworthy. Criticism cannot be constructive unless it is addressed with the source—in Sue's case, her boss. Certainly, we all need to vent or mull problems over with trusted people from time to time, but it is best done without creating third-party triangles.

Criticism is a necessary part of business and leadership. Managers must hold people accountable, judge competencies, develop talent, and deal effectively with behavior that undermines the team. Despite individual differences and an imperfect decoding system for appropriate words, how do you criticize without seeming too critical?

Not long ago I was asked to deliver a very specific message to a CEO from his management team: "Stop calling our ideas 'immature.'" *Immature* perhaps is not a barb on the level of *stupid, irresponsible,* or *thoughtless,* but it is a word that usually offends. Bosses who cannot criticize without also insulting can have measurable negative effects on their organization's bottom line, according to a study conducted by the University of North Carolina at Charlotte. Researchers surveyed 373 Air National Guard members about bosses' abusive actions, such as "tells me my thoughts or feelings are stupid," and they confirmed that employees subjected to these kinds of destructive comments were more likely to perform only the minimum required of them (*New York Times*, December 24, 2002, p. F5).

Meaningful criticism does three things for the person on the receiving end: It helps the person to improve performance while expressing genuine appreciation for and interest in that person's present efforts; it shows the person that his or her performance is worthy of judgment, as opposed to being ignored or unimportant; and it encourages and supports the person so as to build his or her confidence. To make sure that your criticism is helpful information and not another destructive comment, consider these guidelines:

❑ *Think about your message's content and context.* Are you criticizing ideas, values, or behaviors—and not people? What is your motive in criticizing?

❑ *Watch your tone and timing.* Are you speaking in a way that seems helpful and concerned or patronizing and harsh? Are you choosing the best time and setting to criticize someone?

❑ *Do not exaggerate.* When you overstate—such as "Your expense account is putting this department in the poorhouse"—your listener likely will focus on your exaggerated information ("I don't think $204 of expenses for January is putting this department in the poorhouse") instead of your actual point. With hyperbole, instead of driving your point further, your listeners might miss it altogether.

At its best, criticism shows encouragement and support and affirms that the other person's performance matters. And it builds good will. At its worst, criticism breeds fear, distrust, and a lack of confidence.

## "BLAMESTORMING"

Just as criticism must be bridled by adhering to certain guidelines, so should blame, another form of destructive comments.

Wars often exist within companies between divisions and departments; manufacturing blames engineering for designing a product that cannot be built, sales blames marketing for not doing a good job at getting the word out, and every department blames human resources for one thing or another. More layers of blame can exist within each team or department and between individual employees.

The tendency to blame others is an unfortunate reality of human nature, and organizations sometimes promote this culture through their policies and management styles. For example, a company that rewards performance without also recognizing ethical business practices may develop a "succeed at all cost" culture, leading to fierce competition and "blamestorming." A culture of blame is also a large part of America's litigious society; we sue McDonald's for our obesity and their hot coffee and tobacco companies for our addictions. Technology's increasing role in our lives has created more options for blame—in addition to the old standby of malfunctioning alarm clocks, we have computers that lose our documents or fail to send our e-mails.

Somehow, blaming something or someone for what is ultimately our own responsibility makes us feel better. It is usually the easier route, and when everything is someone else's fault, we do not have to face reality. Some people live their whole lives operating like this, never understanding that by not being accountable for their own actions, they are only cheating themselves.

Realize that people who make a habit of "blamestorming" can appear uncooperative, lacking in accountability, self-indulgent, deceitful—and certainly less than credible. More important, "blamestorming" keeps one from taking action and making positive changes for oneself and one's future. Understand that the comfort that comes with finding an outside "cause" for your problems in no way helps you actually solve the problems. More often than not, if something is not going well in our life, if we want something to change or never happen again, we are the only one who can make the difference.

To get control of "blamestorming," follow these guidelines:

1. *Know when to blame and when not to.* Was the situation really out of your control? Is there value in your placing blame elsewhere?

2. *Blame in private and praise in public.* Have a legitimate cause for blaming someone else. You are still responsible for handling it well. Do not embarrass the person in order to make yourself look better. Speak with him or her behind closed doors. If appropriate, agree on terms that will prohibit the problem from coming up again.

3. *Manage misplaced blame.* Do not let others get away with incorrectly placing blame. You do not have to be on a crusade, but make it known when you might disagree with someone else's misplaced blame.

4. *Remember that the first casualty of blame is confidence.* A leader who misplaces blame or harshly blames his or her followers can affect their self-confidence and inhibit performance improvement. And people who make a habit of blaming others negatively affect their own self-confidence because they are missing opportunities to overcome obstacles and make positive changes.

## US VERSUS THEM

Jim, a communications engineer at a major telecommunications company, works from his laptop computer to troubleshoot and resolve customer issues. As long as he has his computer, the solutions can come quickly. Without it, he must call a peer and help him or her investigate a switch he or she is not familiar with, which could take hours—while customers remain without service or with unresolved problems.

"Why would you be without your computer?" I asked Jim.

"Well," he said, "if I don't have it, for sure the techie boys do."

His description of the technical department was purposefully tart, reflecting a sour relationship between Jim's call center and the company's technical department. According to Jim, the technical department is comprised mostly of young males "bursting with computer knowledge and attitude" who feel that they are overworked, underpaid, and very overqualified. "They all think they should be at Microsoft designing and testing the newest software available and making boatloads of money, not babysitting end users and working on antiquated equipment."

In Jim's call center, if you tell someone your laptop is being serviced, you will likely get a standard, sly response: "Oh yeah, what did you do to it now?" According to those at the call center, the technical department never found computer problems to be system-related or due to malfunctioning hardware. Instead, problems were always found to be user-related. When people took their laptops in for repair, they got humiliated with the "techie boys'" litany of questions: "Well, what did you do to it this time? Surf the Internet on some unauthorized sites? Add more 'system-hog' extras? Do your taxes again? Open another e-mail virus?"

"I'd sooner face a root canal, grand jury indictment, or an IRS audit than the ridicule from the techie boys," Jim said. "They get their chuckles watching me explain the symptoms while they interrogate me on where I have been or what I have done to 'their' piece of equipment."

Jim admits that he sometimes just tolerates the computer problems so that he does not have to face the technical department. Consequently, the quality of customer service can be affected, and—since he must do all his status reports and time sheets on the computer—he has to spend several hours in the evening at home getting current when his computer is slow or out for repair.

Jim and his call center and the technical department are involved in an internal conflict that damages the quality of customer service, employee morale, and productivity. While the language of the conflict—the "us-versus-them" destructive comments—is just a symptom of a larger problem, such language also feeds the problem. Comments that group people together and label them—whether by department, level of management, race, age, or socioeconomic status—can limit and divide organizations while at the same time build a false sense of camaraderie. These destructive comments sound like

❑ "Where do those people in finance come up with these ridiculous forms, Mars?"

❑ "Did you see the latest from the marketing department? They must think our customers are stupid."

❑ "This e-mail proves it. The people at the top are clueless when it comes to understanding what we're up against."

❑ "Working with Jerry's team is like walking through a minefield. I'd rather do it myself."

❑ "Oh, of course, when one of the executive team flies, it's first class. But for us peons, it's the back of the bus."

Linda Potter, senior vice president and chief financial officer (CFO) of SunTrust Bank's Central Group in Atlanta, makes it a point to frequently say, "We're all in this together," and believes that us-versus-them mentalities may even indicate a lack of commitment. "Once you choose to work for a company, then you've chosen to be on the same team as everyone else," she said. "If you begin to speak of us versus them, then you may need to reevaluate whether you are truly committed to the company."

A leader who wants to break down the silos in his or her organization needs to help people see how different teams, departments, or divisions interrelate and help to make the whole organization thrive. Groups cannot see themselves as an entity that is not part of a greater whole. Consider putting together a committee of representatives from all the organization's different entities and have them devise strategies for how each group can help the others get their work done. Use language that exhibits a spirit of cooperation and understanding instead of divisiveness. Follow these five principles:

1. *Lose the champ mentality.* Competition within companies can be effective, but be careful when the "win-lose" mentality carries over to who gets what resources, budgetary dollars, status, and so on. Talk openly about departmental discrepancies in senior management meetings and company forums. Educate everyone about the scope of the business, bottom-line issues, the competition, and how and why decisions are made.

2. *Ask and ask again.* Keep the information flowing by beginning or ending every meeting or conference call with questions that beg answers: "What's on your mind?" "What keeps you up at night?" "What do you need to know that you don't?" "What other questions do you have?" Making a habit of such questions also will encourage others to question what they do not understand.

3. *Plug the gap.* Sharing information is critical even in the smallest of organizations, but do not get caught in information overload. Establish an e-mail trail or tag teams that relay information such as product updates, company news, and so on. Hold departments responsible for updating others, and create communications guidelines.

4. *Partner up.* Employees expect bosses to establish strong connections with other leaders in the company, and yet many managers neglect these peer relationships. Nurture and build networks of strong alliances within the organization. Invite a colleague to your weekly meeting for an informal update on his or her area. Schedule informal 30-minute, agenda-free conversations with peers to talk about challenges and ideas. Make these partnerships a priority.

5. *Do not go away mad.* It is not always easy for leaders to buy into an idea they believe is unnecessary or half-baked for "the greater good." Instead of encouraging senior management to vent, most CEOs want to keep moving. If you do not make time for tough conversations when the team is together, what could have been aired and dealt with in the meeting will end up in a snide e-mail or water-cooler conversation. Do not allow people to pretend to agree. Take the time to air disagreements. Work to get comfortable with conflict, and engage everyone.

## WAIT 'TIL YOU HEAR THIS

In the Stone Age, a person's survival depended almost as much on his or her ability to harvest information as it did on gathering nuts and berries, according to Nigel Nicholson, a London Business School professor of organizational behavior. Gossip, Nicholson argued in a *Harvard Business Review* article, has become part of our mental programming ("How Hardwired Is Human Behavior?" by Nigel Nicholson, *Harvard Business Review*, July–August 1998, pp. 135–147). Whether or not you believe in such theories of evolutionary psychology, it is hard to argue with gossip's staying power in our culture. In today's business world, the grapevine twists and turns through every organization, spreading rumors like chaser lights on a Christmas tree.

Gossip can be very tempting. It sometimes slips from one's mouth while one is carelessly chitchatting. Other times it is more calculated, and the people engaging in it are trying to show that they are powerful and in the know. Habitually revealing personal or sensational facts about others can ruin a good reputation—your own. And gossip can seriously undermine workplace relationships.

Gossip also can be an indicator of a workforce that is bored. On a slow day, ears perk up to conversations that begin with something like, "You heard about Al, didn't you?" Gossip also can run rampant in workplace environments in which management is reluctant to address issues head on, leaving employees feeling frustrated because they cannot reach closure on important career-related issues. In these cultures, employees can see coworkers as obstacles rather than team members. Personal talk about someone or an employer has become part of the way we communicate. Especially in work environments in which management is not always forthcoming with information that may affect jobs, people often rely on the informal communication grapevine. Thus the line between ethical business information and unethical gossip has weakened.

But where should you draw the line if you are trying to build credibility? First, determine whether you are participating in this form of destructive comments by asking yourself

1. Do I initiate discussions about coworkers' job performance or personal lives?

2. Do I repeat second-hand information?

3. Do I reveal personal conversations?

4. Do I sometimes offer confidential information to another because I feel that as their "friend," I should tell them?

The unofficial flood of communication may run forever in organizations, but engaging in or encouraging petty and malicious gossip makes one appear untrustworthy and not credible. If you answered yes to any of the preceding questions, then you may have a problem. What many people do not realize is that constantly talking about others—even if your anecdotes sometimes add value and reveal others' good attributes—can make you appear like a gossip. For example, if your story about Jane's uncompromising dedication also reveals, within context, her ensuing divorce and troubled teenager, you have revealed personal information about Jane. Be careful. Weigh your words just as you would if the person being talked about were standing right there with you. You also will want to stop *listening* to gossip if you want to keep your reputation untarnished. Watch out for the coworker who gossips for your benefit: "I just thought you should know."

When having a conversation with someone who begins to talk about another person who is not present—a boss, a colleague, another clerk, or a board member—that person might use phrases like "Let me be honest here . . . . I probably shouldn't say this but . . ." or he or she might assert, "And I'd say the same thing about Sheila if she were here." Such assurances often ring hollow and only leave listeners wondering, "Geez, what does this person say about me when I'm not around?"

If you are a leader, you have responsibilities beyond yourself in controlling gossip. Gossip not only creates a very negative workplace and pits employees against one another, but it also can invite legal repercussions. Managers who share personal information about employees could get sued for defamation, a privacy violation under the Americans with Disabilities Act (revealing a disability to people who do not need to know) or a violation of an employment policy, such as how investigations are conducted "confidentially."

Leaders can take control of gossip in their organizations by doing the following:

❏ *Spread information beyond the top circle.* Arm your managers with information, and let them, rather than just the senior team, deliver messages. This is powerful. Make sure that everyone has access to the same operating metrics, financial data, marketing plans, and sales forecasts. The more people understand what is really going on, the less they have to guess—and gossip—about.

❏ *Do not underestimate their intelligence.* As tempting as it is to gloss over issues because "people won't understand," do not do it. It is a cop out—and it is your job to help everyone understand. Frontline employees may not have engineering degrees, but they will get it if you show them the new product's problems and what the company's challenges are in fixing them. Open communication will quell gossip.

❏ *Go on a weekly tour.* Too much distance between those at the top and those closest to the work is fertile ground for misinformation and unproductive speculation. Do not be inaccessible or unwilling to listen. Go to their work areas and dish dirt. What rumors are they hearing? What's on their minds?

❏ *Take hold of the rumor.* Gossip is likely here to stay, but often rumors can be squelched before they take on a life of their own and zap people's energy and focus. If you get wind of a rumor, assess the negative potential, and then address it immediately, perhaps with 15-minute sessions or informational letters and voice mails with the right audience.

## LOSING OUR SENSES TO GET A LAUGH

While doing some coaching work at the corporate headquarters of a health care provider, I heard a loud voice in the reception area: " Are you ready for a joke?" I peered out through the door of the conference room, and Sue, one of three administrative assistants, made big eyes at me. "What's the difference between a northern zoo and a southern zoo?" a middle-aged male voice asked. I was unable to hear the punch line, and I did not hear any laughter. Later, Sue stopped by and said to me, "That was Dr. Johnson. He does that all the time, but at least today's joke wasn't too . . . you know . . . bad." Sue did not mean "bad" as in "not funny." She meant "distasteful, vulgar, or offensive." Had the doctor been someone I was coaching, I would have told him that while laughter can be good medicine, inappropriate humor in the workplace can wreak havoc on a person's credibility.

Even if you are not the comedian but are only laughing at inappropriate humor in the workplace, your reputation may suffer. Sarah was witness to coworker Jennifer, an engineer at a large telecommunications company, being the butt of a sexist joke; in front of a group of team members, their boss suggested to Jennifer that she wear a leather skirt when meeting with potential customers so that they could get more sales. Sarah felt equal disrespect for her boss and the coworkers who laughed at his comment.

While humor can be a positive force in work relationships, it must be implemented with care and thought. You must use good sense with humor. Research confirms laughter's positive health benefits, and in a stressful workplace, humor can release tension, restore a healthy perspective on a tough situation, open the door for opinions, create a sense of acceptance, and inspire creativity. It also can make others more open to what you have to say. As Judith C. Tingley, Ph.D., writes in *The Power of Indirect Influence:* "When you share some laughter about a common experience, you've already connected on the similarity-bias wavelength and you're in a much better position to then lead the other person where you want her to go" (Amacom, New York, 2001).

The strength of your humor at work is not necessarily measured by clever one-liners. Using humor to your advantage requires having a sense of perspective and seeing humor in tough situations to solve problems and keep stress to a minimum. Instead of making jokes that trivialize or disparage, workplace humor should be about celebrating work. You do not have to remove your funny bone while at the office, but follow these guidelines for making humor appropriate and valuable:

1. *Practice good timing.* Sometimes during a difficult situation people default to telling a joke because they do not know what else to say. This kind of "deflection humor" makes the joker appear weak, lacking in people skills, or callous. This is not to say that humor should be employed only when everyone is happy and good-spirited; attempts to lighten people's moods during stressful times with humor can be very successful and appreciated. During serious times, start slowly with humor. Test the waters and see how others react.

2. *Do not lose your senses.* Having a good sense of humor means that you use your intuition to gauge whether those

around you are distracted or offended by your humor. You do not have to be a mind reader. If your ability to sense whether someone is upset is not fine-tuned, then consider asking, "Everything okay?" when a comment or joke does not get the kind of response you expected. If you find yourself too often saying, "I was just kidding," you likely have a problem.

3. *Do not take yourself too seriously.* One of the safest ways to get a laugh is to joke about yourself. By doing so, you also show others a little humility. You communicate "I'm only human" and a level of self-confidence high enough to open yourself to laughter. You also set the example for others to do the same. But use self-deprecation in moderation, especially when you are around people you do not know. You do not want to appear insecure or clownlike.

4. *Be natural.* Find your own style of humor, one that fits you. If you are trying to be more funny by using Robin Williams' techniques, you may appear like you are trying too hard. Humor has to come naturally.

5. *Do not be offensive.* While laughter is universal, humor is not. You want humor to break down barriers not build them up. Do not tell jokes that are sexist, religious, or racist. If you have to preface a punch line with "I hope this doesn't offend anyone," chances are it probably will. And do not be sarcastic or cynical—negativity is often hard to avoid in humor, but doing so will help you to retain a professional image.

6. *Spread it around.* Help create a work environment that promotes laughter. While you do not want to encourage wasting time by forwarding a lot of e-mail jokes, a particularly funny comic strip posted at the water fountain could lighten someone's step back to his or her desk. Pass out silly party hats at the monthly employee birthday celebration. Make every Friday during the summer months "Hawaiian Shirt Day." Write your monthly staff memo in crazy fonts and colors.

# SARCASTIC TO DOWNRIGHT MEAN

Sarcasm and cynicism often go hand in hand, both revealing an unappealing bitterness that can cripple morale, and they are on the rise in American workplaces.

A number of recent studies show that cynicism is a growing phenomenon in organizational settings. Organizational cynics have negative attitudes about their companies, believing that values of honesty and fairness are often given up for convenience and self-interest and that these things will never change. Some companies and their leaders certainly contribute to cynical attitudes by establishing a history of failed programs aimed at solving morale, production, or quality issues. Although their intentions are often good, leaders may lack the skills necessary to make real changes or have a habit of shifting gears too quickly, jumping from one trendy management technique to another while never really creating a lasting effect.

Do you make sarcastic comments that reflect a cynical attitude about a colleague, your team, or your organization? If so, you may be breeding suspicion and apathy and seriously affecting your credibility. Organizational cynics often behave in ways consistent with their negative beliefs, disparaging those around them and even impeding the success of change agents ("An Upward Feedback Field Experiment," by Leanne E. Atwater, David A. Waldman, and David Atwater, *Personnel Psychology,* Summer 2000, pp. 275–298).

Another kind of destructive comment goes really too far, actually taking on qualities of meanness. "Sometimes she is downright rude," a sales rep said about her boss. It is hard to know what to make of a person who is very caring most of the time and then, for whatever reason, is cruel.

We are all getting a little mean lately, according to C. Leslie Charles, who points to people who practically "snarl 'excuse me'" when someone gets in their way or is pushing others aside. In her book, *Why Is Everyone So Cranky?* Charles illuminates the serious nature of an anger epidemic and cites 10 trends that are making people angry, including competition, compressed time, communication overload, and disconnectedness. It may be impossible to change the complexity of your world, but you can sort through the controllables and uncontrollables. Charles suggests simply taking the time to question what you are doing and why and then choosing the best alternative when you are overwhelmed, overcommitted, or overspent. Ultimately, however, no matter what difficulties you are experiencing, there is no excuse for meanness (*Why Is Everyone So Cranky*, by C. Leslie Charles, Hyperion, New York, 1999).

## EARNING CREDIBILITY
## THROUGH YOUR WORDS

Once people become aware of destructive comments, not saying them anymore is sometimes just a matter of breaking old habits. Try creative accountability. I have suggested to some leaders to make a game out of it by making offenders pay $1 to a pot every time they are caught saying something destructive. Work groups, departments, teams, and entire organizations help one another stop destructive comments at the same time they collect money for a charity, needy family, or the coffee fund. I used this strategy once with my family, and the point stuck. If money is an obstacle, use a horn or a bell.

When Cheryl Bennett, director of customer care at Marco Ophthalmic, Inc., learned that others noticed her destructive comments, she felt "enlightened" and determined to fix it. She announced to her senior executive team that she would not be joining in anymore. Six months later, I asked how she was doing. "I'm not making them, and I feel great about that. But I'm listening to a lot of them!" Even if you cannot change the whole team or organization, breaking your own habits of destructive comments is a worthy accomplishment.

Are you critical or cynical? Do you gossip? Might others perceive you as talking down to them? Saying things without thought or purpose can hurt your credibility, and eliminating destructive comments is challenging. But it can be done. Consider how you might be doling out destructive comments, and resolve to be more mindful of your words.

## DO YOU WATCH YOUR MOUTH?

Using the following scale, rate each expectation of credible leaders in two ways:

How well do you think you are doing at meeting the expectation?

What might others think about how well you are meeting the expectation?

**SCALE:** 1 = significant improvement needed; 2 = slight improvement needed; 3 = skilled/competent; 4 = talented; 5 = outstanding: a role model

| EXPECTATION | HOW DO YOU THINK YOU ARE DOING? | WHAT MIGHT OTHERS THINK? |
|---|---|---|
| Avoids sarcasm and cynicism. | 1 2 3 4 5 | 1 2 3 4 5 |
| Avoids acting arrogant or "talking down" to people. | 1 2 3 4 5 | 1 2 3 4 5 |
| Displays an appropriate sense of humor. | 1 2 3 4 5 | 1 2 3 4 5 |
| Avoids derogatory comments that group people by gender, race, culture, age, etc. | 1 2 3 4 5 | 1 2 3 4 5 |
| Rarely says a bad thing about anyone. | 1 2 3 4 5 | 1 2 3 4 5 |
| Never criticizes someone in front of others. | 1 2 3 4 5 | 1 2 3 4 5 |

| Avoids destructive comments about other parts of the organization. | 1 2 3 4 5 | 1 2 3 4 5 |
| Does not contribute to or promote workplace gossip. | 1 2 3 4 5 | 1 2 3 4 5 |
| Discourages "us-versus-them" attitudes. | 1 2 3 4 5 | 1 2 3 4 5 |
| Confronts issues directly with those involved (avoids third-party triangles). | 1 2 3 4 5 | 1 2 3 4 5 |

**MY SCORES:**

*Scoring yourself:* Add your total for each column. A single column score of 45 to 50 suggests that you are doing an exceptional job and meeting others' expectations of someone who avoids destructive comments. A column score of 37 to 44 indicates that you have some areas for improvement; on issues as important as these, I believe leaders should strive to be "outstanding: a role model." Below 37 indicates a danger area, and you may be chipping away at your credibility. A discrepancy of more than 11 points between the two column totals indicates a possible gap in perception worth investigating. If your "How do you think you are doing?" score is higher than your "What might others think?" score, your intentions may be better than your actions. If your "What might others think?" score is higher, you may not be giving yourself enough credit for a job well done.

# CHAPTER 10

# Don't Hold Your Applause

*The people we interviewed from good-to-great companies clearly loved what they did, largely because they loved who they did it with.*

—Jim Collins, AUTHOR OF *GOOD TO GREAT: WHY SOME COMPANIES MAKE THE LEAP . . . AND OTHERS DON'T*

Jimmy Yancey has been reporting to Jim Blanchard for 33 years. It is a rare, long, and successful relationship in a working world where even 5-year relationships with a manager are uncommon. In tandem since 1970, Yancey and Blanchard have helped grow Synovus from one bank in Columbus, Georgia, to a more than $19 billion diversified financial services company including 40 banks in 5 states and an 81.1 percent stake in a payment processing business. Yancey began as a commercial lending officer and is now president and chief operating officer (COO); Blanchard started as the company's top executive (when Synovus was one bank in Columbus) and remains at the head of the table today. "I always tell him that one of his weaknesses is that he's never known the thrill of being promoted," Yancey jokes.

At the heart of their success are core values of care for one another and respect. "[Blanchard] has high expectations, but I've always come away with the sense that he cares about me and my growth," Yancey told me. These same values are spread throughout Synovus' organization and culture. All Synovus managers are trained in and expected to follow the company's "Leadership Expectations" model:

1. *Live the values.* Among them are applying the "Golden Rule," taking 100 percent responsibility, valuing differences, walking the talk, and having fun.

2. *Share the vision.* Yancey explains that managers at all levels are responsible for communicating Synovus' vision.

3. *Make others successful.* Synovus leaders are charged with facilitating individual development, being accessible, and rewarding and recognizing people.

4. *Manage the business.* This is the nuts and bolts of getting the job done, Yancey says. Expectations include executing results within budget, thinking twice, and serving with high energy.

The model is one way Synovus ensures that its 11,400 team members feel valued. And certainly in that regard it appears to work—in 2003, Synovus was named number 9 on *Fortune*'s list of "Best Companies to Work For" in America.

In order for leaders to be successful at influencing and motivating people, their followers must have a solid answer to the question: Do you care about *me?* Leaders must visibly show followers that, yes, they do care, and this is done by developing the followers, recognizing them, and seeking to know and understand them.

While showing value for employees has lasting bottom-line benefits in morale, quality, and productivity, a leader should not be motivated to demonstrate care and value for the organization's benefit alone. Such a narrow view undermines the formula and ultimately provides a disappointing answer to the individual follower's aforementioned question: Do you care about *me?* True leadership is built on a kind of social contract that says, "Follow me, and I promise that I will help you to succeed." When this contract is not honored, the motivation behind a leader's strategy of transparency is put to question, and followers are led to wonder about hidden agendas.

As a leader, are you doing enough to show your followers that you care about them?

___ I know one aspect of work each of my people is dying to learn to do.

___ I am aware of what frustrates each person about the work he or she does.

___ I push people to do things when I think they are ready even if they do not think they are.

___ I set stretch goals with my people.

___ I share what I have learned in meetings with my staff.

___ I regularly give them articles or books to read about leadership.

___ I encourage them to tell their people about our company's messages instead of me always doing it.

___ I attend their departmental meetings often.

___ I use informal and impromptu times to talk with each person about the challenges of his or her work.

___ I am often in the cafeteria or in people's offices, encouraging people to ask me questions so that I can learn what is important to them.

___ Learning is a priority for me, and I encourage others to learn.

___ I make a point to share news about our industry and the marketplace.

___ I sometimes put people in a conference room and give them a problem to solve.

___ I encourage people to learn about other parts of the business.

____I encourage team members to learn from one another.

____I frequently turn an entire project over to a team member and tell him or her to run with it.

____I always try to understand what my people are up against.

____I consistently recognize individual efforts.

## DEVELOP INDIVIDUALS, NOT JUST TEAMS

It was during college that Scott McKoin, now a 39-year-old Citigroup executive, learned that leaders should not use a one-size-fits-all approach to developing and motivating followers. As a basketball player at the University of Texas at San Antonio, McKoin, along with his other teammates, prepared for a new season with a "star" freshman player, an All-American who "dominated in each practice," McKoin said. Yet, when the first game was played, the team's new star seemed "lost on the court," took bad shots, and generally played surprisingly poorly. In order to learn how to get results from each team member, especially the new player who had disappointed everyone, McKoin's coach put the team through extensive personality profiling and self-assessments, learning their strengths and weaknesses, and there were many social gatherings where the coach learned about each individual's background and values. "He learned what made each of us tick," McKoin said. And then the coach used his new knowledge in deciding how to develop each player. The All-American, for example, seemed to perform worse if the coach kept bringing to attention his problem areas—he couldn't handle the pressure of the crowds, fanfare, and referee—so that player got more positive reinforcement. Other players responded better to constructive criticism. "Everybody on the team wanted to do well—that was a given," McKoin said. "But the coach treated people differently to achieve the same results."

Today McKoin has integrated the same strategy into his leadership style as managing director of the western division of CitiFinancial's $10 billion auto finance group. He manages each of his six direct reports according to their individual goals, strengths, and weaknesses.

A leader's mission to help his or her team to grow begins with identifying the capabilities and drivers of his or her people; learning their strengths, weaknesses, and needs; and knowing what they seek to achieve in their careers. When asked whether their leaders demonstrate appreciation of others' concerns, feelings, motives, needs and competencies, 79 percent of 7107 executives did not give their leaders the highest rating. And 91 percent of those executives' leaders actually agreed.

Yet this is vital and necessary information for leaders who say that they want to develop their followers. Once leaders know their team members' talents, motivations, and deficiencies, then they can match them up with the projects, challenges, and resources that will help them to succeed. As a leader, you need to know the following about your followers:

❏ What do they want from their work besides money?

❏ What aren't they getting?

❏ What are their personal objectives for their career?

❏ What are their aspirations?

❏ What would help them to love their work?

❏ What kinds of tasks and responsibilities would they like to have at work that they do not presently have?

❑ What skills do they need in order to perform those tasks and responsibilities successfully?

❑ What do they want to learn more about?

❑ What is something I do that they would like to learn?

❑ What are they afraid of?

❑ What could they do to overcome that fear?

In hunting down the answers to these questions, realize that the process will take time and likely will be ongoing. People and workplaces are constantly changing, so 4-month-old information about an employee's goals and weaknesses may be obsolete. Whether through frequent conversations or formal personality profiling, seek the answers in ways that fit your leadership style and your organization's culture.

Pam Bilbrey, senior vice president of corporate development for Baptist Health Care (BHC), which ranked number 10 on *Fortune*'s 2002 list of the nation's "Best Companies to Work For," commits a lot of time to developing each of her eight direct reports. When Bilbrey asked one of them, Rose Slade, what she envisioned for her career, Bilbrey learned that Slade wanted to do something different than her current role as director of HealthSource, a call-in service offered by BHC to consumers. Trained as a nurse, Slade was interested in marketing data analysis, which required skills that Slade not only did not have but also really did not need in her current position. Through 6 months of strategizing, Bilbrey and Slade developed a win-win plan for BHC and Slade. To begin acquiring the marketing data analysis skills she ultimately wanted, Slade enrolled in an evening MBA program. Meanwhile, Bilbrey found a learning opportunity within BHC for Slade, who, while maintaining her current responsibilities, worked on a marketing data analysis project in another area of BHC. Slade's new skills and knowledge ultimately worked to BHC's advantage. While HealthSource had never produced revenues (it was an investment BHC made to better serve its customers), Slade found a creative way to package some of the call center's services, sell them to other organizations, and tap into an income source for BHC.

Bilbrey's reputation for helping others succeed stretches beyond her own team, and she regularly receives calls from people in other areas of BHC asking for advice and 20 to 30 minutes of her time. One young man, a sports marketer, had only 16 months left before his contract was up, and because the sports market had matured and BHC wanted to downsize its sports marketing program, his contract would not be renewed. Bilbrey spent time mentoring him and helping him to identify his strengths and interests, and eventually he took a position within the fundraising division of BHC. Because of Bilbrey's investment in the young man, he was able to understand that BHC could still fit his needs, and BHC retained a solid performer. "I look for him to move up in the organization," Bilbrey said. "He is also very loyal to Baptist and is one of our greatest supporters in the community."

One of a manager's fundamental tasks is to provide the tools and conditions necessary for people to grow in their work, yet some managers rarely look beyond their own needs and often view their team members as means to an end. Again, followers must believe that their leaders truly care about them; and leaders must translate their words—"I'm here to help. If you succeed, I succeed. I want you to eventually take my place"—into visible actions. Consider ways that leaders can move beyond mere intentions and show a measurable interest in helping their followers succeed:

*Share the baton.* What tasks are you performing that someone else could learn to do and grow from? Why does Jim always go to the annual industry meeting? Can someone else go instead? Can John help Linda polish her presentation skills so that she can do the opening overview at the quarterly meeting? There are always opportunities to give your followers developmental challenges, and by doing so, you make "on-the-job training" a reality.

Mike Harreld, CFO of Georgia Power Company, a subsidiary of Southern Company, believes that sharing his

responsibilities is one of the best ways to develop his followers. "I tell them I won't be in the batter's box knock-
ing them out of the park anymore—they will," Harreld
said. "I'll be in the dugout with the line-up card, watching them hit the runs." Having worked at Southern Company for more than 20 years, Harreld feels that it is his
duty as one of the organization's experienced leaders to
allow his five direct reports to stretch into his role sometimes. Thus, for instance, they may be the ones standing
in front of the team of managing officers explaining the
financial numbers; doing so may have "scared them a bit
at first," but they have become accustomed to the task,
Harreld said. He also might take one or two of his direct
reports along with him when he lunches with his own
boss. In addition to pushing them to develop, Harreld's
approach sends a loud message that he has confidence in
them and thinks them vital to his success.

*Be resource-rich.* Helping your followers grow in their careers
does not have to begin and end with you alone. Many
companies have excellent programs to help their employees learn and develop talents—mentors or learning partners, access to community leadership programs,
cross-training opportunities, and in-house universities. As
a leader, you should know what is available and what it
takes to get your people involved.

*Teach them to hunt.* Encourage your followers to constantly
seek out information that could prove valuable and to
never be out of touch with their internal or external customers. Make arrangements for one of your team members to meet with a peer in a different part of the
organization for an interview or attend another department's weekly meeting. He or she will increase his or her
knowledge about the business and learn to see things
from others' perspectives. Send a customer service rep out
on a call with a sales rep; they both probably will learn
something.

*Create attack teams.* Give your group a problem, and let them go at it. Describe your biggest challenge, and ask for solutions. Or include a problem-solving space on the agenda of your weekly meeting, allowing team members to share an issue they are having difficulty with and letting other members suggest strategies for handling it. Set a time limit so the team does not get bogged down in the process or get too far off on a tangent.

Ken Carty, director of global procurement at Coca-Cola Company, builds his followers' confidence and skill sets by expecting their full participation in problem solving. Once, when turf issues and various organizational changes had his 14-member team stalled in performance, he took them all off their jobs and sent them to a conference room at an Atlanta Ritz Carlton for a 2-day meeting, which I facilitated. Their mission: Redesign their workflow and be prepared to present the new plan on Friday. Ken purposefully did not attend the meeting. "I can't do it for them—only they can," he said. While some of the team members at first were doubtful that they could accomplish the task, all felt great satisfaction when they reached a successful conclusion at the end of the second day.

*Do not lose sight of the individual.* Remember that development is most effective when it is matched with a follower's growth areas and personal goals. A leader who works hard in the design phase of his or her team's development, staying in tune with strengths, weaknesses, and desires, and matches his or her strategies with individuals likely will see bigger results.

## RECOGNIZE THEIR VICTORIES

Ken Carty, the Coca-Cola leader I mentioned earlier, has a salt-of-the-earth, unassuming way about him that his followers appreciate. And they acknowledge his commitment to honesty, his stellar industry knowledge, and his decision-making skills. After Ken was selected to head the company's global procurement function, we talked about his leadership skills and what might lie ahead for him. I expressed concern about his ability to motivate and infuse excitement in the troops by recognizing their strengths and victories, small and large. With Ken's increasing prominence as a leader and his company's recent reorganization, offering consistent recognition and praise was in many ways crucial to morale. Ken admitted that he did a pretty good job of recognizing others' strengths and contributions at performance evaluation time, but he said that he did not praise people on a regular basis.

I cautioned him against running right out and slapping people on the back, saying, "Good job."

"That's not your style," I said. "Find your own way, one that's comfortable for you, and be sincere about it. But make it happen."

Later Ken told me that he had kicked off his first meeting for his group with a 3-hour presentation on the organization's goals and future vision. During that presentation, he recognized 67 different people for their contributions, commitment, follow-through, or perseverance. He did not take an awards-ceremony approach; no one was asked to stand and be applauded. He simply wove the success stories into his presentation, making each one relevant to the content. Preparing the presentation took a lot of time and work, Ken said, because he had to learn details about the contributions of individual members. But the results were incredibly effective.

"It was one of the most powerful presentations I've ever seen," one of Ken's direct reports said. "It was powerful because some of the people he recognized had no idea that he even knew about what was going on in their work."

Another said: "It was the quiet way he chose to do it. It was his own way. That's what made it so great."

Leaders who care about their followers and invest the time to learn what is important to them know that people yearn for recognition and that cash is not king. People who do great work are glad to get paid, but they do not do the work for the paycheck alone.

In a 360-degree survey, a small-business CEO in Philadelphia scored himself high on "positive recognition," whereas all 11 of his direct reports scored him low. One employee, in his middle fifties, told me: "Positive recognition? I'm thrilled when he says hello to me." Followers of other neglectful leaders have similar comments:

❏ "I don't feel rewarded, and it's not just about monetary rewards. It's about making me feel that my work is important."

❏ "She seems to have a real knack for devaluing people and their projects."

❏ "He makes us feel like we're not cutting it."

Leaders who take the time to recognize followers' efforts and successes are described like this:

❏ "He acknowledges a job well done."

❏ "I appreciate the environment Karla has created, and I enjoy coming to work everyday. She recognizes me when I'm successful and creates opportunities to have my work seen by others."

❏ "Cindy is very gracious and consistent in her recognition of good work."

❏ "John is quick to say 'Thank you.'"

❏ "Joe will drop me a note to let me know I've done a good job. I very much appreciate that."

❏ "Emily takes time to personally recognize and reward team members."

Unfortunately, most leaders do not receive these comments from their direct reports. In fact, most employees feel that their managers have great room for improvement in recognizing achievements.

Why don't leaders make this a priority?

1. I'm too busy.

2. Why should I compliment someone for doing good work? It's their job. That's what they get paid for.

3. I don't see anything to recognize people for.

4. If I compliment one, the others will think I'm playing favorites.

5. They might get a big head and stop doing their work.

6. I don't need a pat on the back, and I don't think they really care about it either.

7. I know it's important, but I forget.

8. When people say they want reward and recognition, I think they mean more money.

9. If I compliment people a lot, I might have a problem when performance appraisal time comes around—they'll expect top ratings.

Number six comes up a lot. Successful high achievers are often self-starters and intrinsically motivated. If they get a pat on the back, great; if not, no big deal. These are people who will work hard and continually strive for excellence with or without recognition and who do not quite understand others' need for it. Often, however, when I encourage them to look deeper, they remember a time a compliment was very meaningful or they recall a letter they have kept over the years that told them, "You made a difference to me," or "You're one of the smartest people I know."

Despite plenty of studies that prove the bottom-line benefits and a host of books that give ideas about how to do it, positively recognizing employees continues to be one of the most undervalued and underused management practices. And it does not have to cost a dime.

Many leaders *think* they do a great job at giving positive feedback and are surprised when their direct reports say otherwise. In a coaching session with Don, a senior vice president at a telecommunications company, he struggled to understand how his team rated him a 3.2 out of 5 on positively recognizing people.

"Barbara, I do it," he said.

"How do you think your children or your wife would rate you on positive recognition?" I asked, explaining that when we are exploring behaviors, we sometimes can translate them from personal life to professional life.

Don said that his son was 30, out of the house, and working in Chicago; then he picked up the phone and called his wife.

"Mariette," he said, "there's a woman in my office who wants to ask you a question."

With a nod from Don, I asked Mariette how, on a scale from 1 to 5, she would rate her husband on positively recognizing her as a partner in their marriage. It was quiet for what seemed like a long time. Don looked at me, and I looked at him. We looked at the telephone.

Finally, Mariette said, "I would give him a 3."

Don winced.

Mariette's score helped Don own the behavior, and we immediately worked on a plan for improvement. A year later, in a subsequent 360-degree survey, his overall feedback score was significantly improved.

Leaders sometimes genuinely try to send the message that they value their followers' achievements and contributions, yet their messages are not heard. It may be difficult for employees to see a connection between recognition for their individual work and the box of bagels that's left for everyone or a banner in the break room that applauds hard work. While group praise usually is appreciated and helps to build a team spirit, employees also want recognition for their individual performance directly from their leader.

Yet, while some leaders excel at recognizing groups of people, most miss the mark in letting individuals feel valued for their own contribution. In November 2002, Baptist Health Care surveyed 1800 employees, asking them about their individual preferences for reward and recognition. Answers—

which even outline an employee's favorite candy bar, restaurant, and pizza toppings—are kept on the company's intranet site, and employees can change their answers at any time. Managers are expected to know their team members' preferences and match reward and recognition to each individual.

When David Marco hands out the "President's Award" at his company's annual banquet, he does much more than offer a plaque and round of applause. The employees of Marco Ophthalmic, a Jacksonville, Florida-based provider of vision diagnostic equipment, have come to expect president and CEO Marco to present the top leadership award with a lengthy profile of the individual, accompanied by a slide show of pictures he received from the person's parents after he interviewed them. When Marco discovered that the 2002 winner, Andy Millsom, valued his family above all and even involved them in helping him achieve his sales goals—Millsom's goals were posted in various places around his house, and his children were known to ask their father, "How much did you sell today, Daddy?"—Marco surprised Millsom by flying his wife in from California for the banquet (the kids were in school). In his speech, Marco said: "I know that your family is important to you, because they told me so. And I know that more than anything you wish they were here. And one of them is." Millsom's wife appeared on stage and gave a speech to the employees about her husband before giving him the award.

"The presentation really sent a message that Marco truly values people," said David Gurvis, chief operating officer for Marco Ophthalmic. "It was the topic of discussion during the whole 2-day meeting."

Start looking around for opportunities to recognize people. Pick up the phone and call one of your sales reps to acknowledge his or her effort in getting this month's numbers back up. When you walk out of Monday's meeting, tell your colleague, "You know, I appreciated that question you asked. I really thought that was important." There's no one-size-fits-all formula to recognizing others. The only hard-fast rules are that you are sincere and consistent in your efforts. Also consider the following points:

*Longhand does it every time.* We connect to a message of words crafted with another's own hand. Nothing replaces the feeling of reading a handwritten note from your boss. Sometimes the words do not even mean as much as knowing that he or she took the time and made the effort. In Baptist Health Care's survey, the company found that a written note of appreciation was one of its employees' most preferred ways of being recognized.

*Work it into daily interactions.* An unrehearsed moment of appreciation may have a more lasting effect than a loud "Thank you" said into the microphone at the quarterly awards meeting. A minute in the hall or an impromptu duck into another's office with a quick comment—"You did that well," "I heard great things about you," or "You keep getting better"—can make a big impact.

*If you are not sure how they want to be recognized, ask.* This goes back to what we talked about earlier. A leader should know how each follower defines meaningful praise and recognition. For example, some people actually cringe at public praise. In Baptist Health Care's survey, the company found that 84 percent of employees wanted verbal thanks that was given privately, whereas only 17 percent said they preferred public praise.

*You probably cannot overdo it.* I have never met a person who said their boss recognizes them too much.

## PRACTICE TOUGH EMPATHY

For 25 years Margery Miller has run her Dallas-based manufacturers' representative firm for the commercial food service equipment industry with a high priority placed on both the professional and personal development of her 11 employees. "They have to go together," Miller told me. "If you're not growing as an individual, both in your career and in your personal life, you're not going to help my company grow." In

1992, Dave, the inside sales member who had been Miller's top performer for almost a decade, began slipping in performance, and his sales flattened. After spending some time with Dave, Miller realized that his personal life had been suffering because he had been placing such a high priority on his career. "The lack of balance was diminishing for him, and it was negatively affecting his work," she said. Dave needed to attend to more personal issues in order for his work success to return. For several years Miller had been operating a consulting business outside her rep firm, coaching people on self-awareness and personal development, and she offered her services to Dave at no cost. After working together to reinstate some balance in Dave's life, his work turnaround began, and since 1994, Dave's sales have "skyrocketed"; now with the company almost 20 years, Dave consistently surpasses his sales goals, and he is back to being the company's top performer. Said Miller, "He's also a more mature and effective person now, and he contributes more to the company by really taking a lead in helping others learn."

Leaders who demonstrate appreciation and understanding for their followers' needs and feelings are more likely to build strong, loyal relationships and successful teams. Focusing exclusively on business goals and operational strategies neglects what is equally important—engaging with people individually and inspiring commitment and enthusiasm. Showing empathy while still recognizing the tasks at hand can be a powerful way to connect with people at work. When a peers says, "I know that was tough for you," after your proposal was dissected and trashed, or when your boss listens attentively as you explain what you are up against in meeting your numbers—even though he or she still holds you to meeting those numbers—you feel acknowledged and perhaps understood. Leaders who are empathetic do not take on their people's troubles, but they do take on their feelings.

As vice president of vocational services for Pensacola, Florida–based Lakeview Center, Inc., a mental health services company, Rich Gilmartin is responsible for more than 820 employees in 5 states. When funding was lost for a mentoring program for welfare mothers, 8 people were slated to lose their jobs, and Gilmartin knew this 3 months before the layoffs were to occur. He had to make a choice: Tell the 8 employees just before their last day, giving them minimum notice; or tell them immediately, hoping that they would not bail out before the 3 months were up. Gilmartin put himself in their shoes, decided to give them the full 90 days to prepare, and notified them in person of what was to come. While one did lose enthusiasm, most of the employees continued to work hard until the end. Although Gilmartin had already proven empathetic to his followers, in hindsight he said that he should have done even more. "If I had to do it over again," he said, "I would have stayed around (at their facility) for a couple of days in case they wanted to stop by and talk, and I would have met with them individually during the 3 months to see how they were doing."

By thinking ahead and anticipating responses, you can be better prepared to show people that you understand their needs and concerns. If time allows, ask yourself these questions before deciding how to handle sensitive situations:

❑ How might I feel if it were me?

❑ What would I want others to say to me?

❑ How would I like to be treated?

When leaders are able to show a sincere capacity and desire to understand what others are up against, they visibly demonstrate they care and build more trusting relationships.

Amelia Tess Thornton, former chief administrative officer of Hyperion Solutions, a $500 million performance management software company, could have lapsed into corporate speak when an employee questioned her after the terrorist attacks on September 11, 2001. Tess Thornton was the first officer from the Sunnyvale, California, headquarters to visit the satellite office in Stamford, Connecticut, after the tragedies. As was typical of Tess Thornton, she told everyone as she walked through the Stamford site that she would be in the cafeteria for lunch if they wanted to talk. About 60 people did. Many questions centered on the national tragedy, including one employee's question, "Has our company strategy changed since September 11?" Tess Thornton quickly realized that there was an emotional disconnect between the Hyperion employees in Connecticut, who were closer to the tragedy both geographically and emotionally in that many had friends and relatives who had been affected, and those in Hyperion's California offices. "In California, although we certainly looked at it as a national tragedy and a horrible thing, we just weren't as close to it as people on the East Coast," Tess said. She realized that although she probably had expected to show up and express empathy to the East Coast team, she really was not capable of offering it. She chose honesty: "I just stopped and said, 'I just want to acknowledge that we probably don't understand what you're going through, and please forgive us if we're insensitive or if I say something that doesn't make sense to you.'" The employees appreciated her clear desire to understand and appreciated even more her honest words.

Because they must influence a number of people in order to be effective, leaders must work hard to fine-tune their intuitive skills so that they can read a team, not just an individual. Group dynamics can complicate issues. Leaders must be able to have a sense of what emotions are bubbling under that conference table. Many leaders have experienced a team meeting where everyone seemed to agree, even said they were on board, and then disengaged or sabotaged the new initiative when they left the room. I have watched leaders completely misread a group. In debriefing, they will say, "They love my new idea for performance pay, don't they?" And yet, as a more objective party, I perceived that they hated it.

A leader who is adept at sensing others' feelings will be more likely to establish more connected, stronger relationships and will have a keen understanding of where his or her team stands on important issues. If your ability to read your group needs tuning, here are some ideas to get started:

1. *Do not respond so quickly to ideas that are different from yours.* If someone says, "I don't see it that way at all," or "There's a lot more to this than you think," do not quickly launch into trying to convince him or her of your way. Take some time to discover what he or she is thinking and why.

2. *Ask people what they are feeling.* It is hard at times to read people, so ask. "How do you feel about that?" "What kinds of feelings might you have if that happened?" You will get better understanding emotions as you listen to people express them. You also will have more information that may be helpful to you in the future. If they express—"I might not be too happy about changing that procedure"— and the procedure changes, you will be able to go back and express concern. "How are you doing with all this?"

3. *Change roles in your meetings.* It is very difficult to monitor the emotional landscape of teams, especially when you are leading the meeting. Do not lead all your meetings. Let someone else run a meeting (a team member or an outside facilitator, for example), or run part of it and let others be in charge for a portion. Also, you could have a coach, boss, or peer, if they are astute in group dynamics, observe a meeting and debrief with you. When you are out of the lead role, ask yourself, "What might Larry be thinking? Stacy? Who looks bored? Excited? Who's engaged and who isn't?" Look for points in the meeting where the group dynamics seem to shift. What happened to make the energy disappear?

4. *Make an emotional guess.* When you are trying to develop an intuitive sense, do not be afraid of being wrong. You can get a lot of information when you offer up your best shot. Guess: "You seem upset." Response: "I'm not upset. I'm mad as hell." Guess: "You seem pleased about that." Response: "Well I was in the beginning, but now I'm getting nervous." Guess: "I'm sensing that everyone's tired of talking about this." Response: "No, we need to have this discussion."

## VALUING OTHERS

One leader, Rob, had this feedback from one of his peers: "The one thing Rob could do better as a leader is to pay attention to his staff. From personal observation and experience, at times Rob's staff feels left out, not important, and left on the 'back burner.'"

When it comes to helping your followers succeed, recognizing them, and seeking to understand them, if you have any of the following thoughts, you might need to consider whether your heart's in the job:

1. I can't afford the time.

2. I don't think that's part of my role.

3. I can't promote them, so what's the point?

4. I don't know how to teach people to achieve higher performance.

5. This feels too soft to me.

6. Coaching people is just the latest new management fad.

7. I'm not sure they are capable of learning new things.

8. Each person is responsible for his or her own growth and development.

9. If I let them learn, they might become great and get my job.

10. Money is still the best motivator.

Remember, if you want to be perceived as a credible leader, you must abide by the contract that says, "Follow me, and I promise that I will help you succeed." If you do not seek to understand and help your followers, your agenda may be questioned. Ultimately, people do not want to work for someone who just plays the role of a manager, merely living up to the obligations of the job. They want someone who is committed to and cares passionately about the work and the people.

# DO OTHERS THINK YOU CARE ABOUT THEM?

Using the following scale, rate each expectation of credible leaders in two ways:

How well do you think you are doing at meeting the expectation?

What might others think about how well you are meeting the expectation?

**SCALE:** 1 = significant improvement needed; 2 = slight improvement needed; 3 = skilled/competent; 4 = talented; 5 = outstanding: a role model

| EXPECTATION | HOW DO YOU THINK YOU ARE DOING? | WHAT MIGHT OTHERS THINK? |
| --- | --- | --- |
| Demonstrates appreciation of others' concerns, feelings, and needs. | 1 2 3 4 5 | 1 2 3 4 5 |
| Treats others as partners, not competitors. | 1 2 3 4 5 | 1 2 3 4 5 |
| Delegates in a way that leverages strengths and uses others' competencies. | 1 2 3 4 5 | 1 2 3 4 5 |
| Seeks to recognize others in new and different ways. | 1 2 3 4 5 | 1 2 3 4 5 |
| Determines what motivates others. | 1 2 3 4 5 | 1 2 3 4 5 |
| Coaches people to strive for their highest potential. | 1 2 3 4 5 | 1 2 3 4 5 |
| Avoids playing favorites. | 1 2 3 4 5 | 1 2 3 4 5 |

Promotes a culture of recognition    1 2 3 4 5    1 2 3 4 5
and appreciation.

**MY SCORES:**

*Scoring yourself:* Add your total for each column. A single column score of 36 to 40 suggests that you are doing an exceptional job and meeting others' expectations of a leader who values people. A column score of 30 to 35 indicates that you have some areas for improvement; on issues as important as these, I believe leaders should strive to be "outstanding: a role model." Below 30 indicates a danger area, and you may be chipping away at your credibility. A discrepancy of more than 9 points between the two column totals indicates a possible gap in perception worth investigating. If your "How do you think you are doing?" score is higher than your "What might others think?" score, your intentions may be better than your actions. If your "What might others think?" score is higher, you may not be giving yourself enough credit for a job well done.

# Epilogue

O ne of the risks inherent in writing a book such as this is that the topic—in this case transparent leadership that builds credibility—may seem easy or at least simple. Thus we feel compelled to end with a clarification: Transparent leadership, in practice, is neither easy nor simple. It can be hard, painful, exhausting, and even risky. Leaders often find themselves in complex situations—people become unpredictable, changes explode one's best intentions, and business strategies necessary for survival require outrageous speed over rough terrain for long periods of time. Adding transparency to the leadership mix may seem a daunting task.

Indeed, keeping a promise, telling the truth, and delivering bad news well are very difficult to do. Facing people with mistakes and asking for constructive criticism are also challenging tasks, certainly ones that will not be relished. However, for those leaders who are willing, there are valuable rewards.

More than ever, organizations need transparent leaders. People want a boss with depth and conviction. They want to see their leader's credibility in action. Each day and every organizational juncture provides opportunities to be transparent and build credibility. The right choices create defining moments that will lead you toward a solid reputation, strong relationships, and a winning performance. A wrong choice can strip you or your organization of credibility. And like trust, credibility is difficult to earn back.

If you have read this book, you now know that transparent leadership that strengthens credibility requires one to tune into a sense of how much and what information others can handle effectively and to deliver that information in honorable, caring, and respectful ways. This kind of leadership takes a lot of courage and know-how. The courage must come from within, whereas the know-how comes from sources outside yourself. This book was a good start. What's next? How will you determine what changes to make and how to make those changes last?

We suggest that you begin by gathering information about your current performance level. A 360-degree assessment is a good way to do this. Then, based on the information you receive, make a plan for improvement, work the plan, and consistently follow up. When leaders do these things and continue to repeat the process, they experience positive results and sustained change. Great leaders are responsibly transparent. They demonstrate integrity, generate trust, and communicate values. When leaders tap into transparency that strengthens credibility, they create other leaders, energize followers, and increase loyalty, and the authenticity of the entire organization is felt inside and out.

To learn more about our ongoing work, we encourage you to join our circle of interest at *www.transparencyedge.com.* Our Web site offers additional reading and case studies and information about our assessments, learning programs, and other resources.

Finally, we wish you and your organization all the credibility, satisfaction, and success that can come from transparent leadership.

# Data Analysis

The highlighted statistics in this book were derived using data from a database of approximately 16,000 people who participated in 360-degree assessments developed and administered by Assessment Plus, an Atlanta-based firm with worldwide clients and an affiliation with the University of Georgia, where graduate students are sometimes tapped to conduct applied research on clients' data. Assessment Plus and its team of organizational psychologists and coaches worked with us to develop *Transparency Edge 360™*, a leadership inventory that provides feedback on the nine behaviors outlined in this book.

We asked Assessment Plus a few questions aimed at helping readers further understand the data and the 360-degree assessment process. Our questions and their answers follow.

## WHO IS REPRESENTED IN THE DATABASE?

The database used to provide research in this book consists primarily of senior- and upper-level management in Fortune 500 organizations from various industries as well as government agencies. Some of the industries represented in this database include (but are not limited to) pharmaceuticals, telecommunications, technology, consumer products, and manufacturing. The participants and raters who provided data are located in various geographic locations throughout the world.

## HOW WERE THE ASSESSMENT ITEMS DEVELOPED?

Assessment Plus has been developing customized assessments for organizations for almost 20 years. During this time, we have collaborated with industrial and organizational psychologists, measurement experts, statisticians, and leaders within these organizations to ensure that the items we are using are psychometrically accurate, as well as practical and meaningful. Our years of experience and research contribute to the comprehensive bank of items we use, as well as newly customized items used for specific functions, organizations, or industries. Our goal is to develop and use items that are specific, meaningful, measurable, and result in feedback that can be used to help identify an individual's strengths and developmental areas.

## WHAT EXACTLY IS A 360-DEGREE ASSESSMENT AND HOW IS IT TYPICALLY USED?

Feedback is a critical element in a person's professional and personal development. Thus 360-degree feedback offers a unique opportunity for leaders to find out how their direct reports, their colleagues, their internal and external customers, and their managers perceive their effectiveness in various areas. By soliciting this feedback from the various rater groups, it gives the leader a more complete view of his or her behavior, strengths, and developmental areas. This type of feedback enables a manager to leverage the areas that are perceived to be strengths and target the developmental areas for improvement.

In the early 1950s, there was a wide acceptance and implementation of management by objectives, which helped formalize the feedback process. Individuals were then able to work with their managers to establish and meet specific targets that would benefit them as well as their organization. It also was discovered that both productivity and job satisfaction improved when people received regular feedback relating to their performance targets. This led to more structured performance reviews in most organizations.

One disadvantage to the performance review just described is that it offers a limited perspective. Typically, the manager is more concerned with the results rather than how the results were achieved, and evaluations often are based solely on financial results. This leads to a performance review that is less than complete. During the early 1970s, other approaches to feedback were explored, and research substantiated that feedback from direct reports was very valuable in the ongoing development and leadership effectiveness of managers. IBM was one of the first organizations to implement a 360-degree process over 35 years ago, and the company still uses the process as part of its leadership development initiatives.

Research since the 1980s has indicated that gathering feedback from multiple perspectives gives an even more complete picture of a manager's effectiveness. Raters such as work teams, colleagues, and customers are affected by the behavior of a manager and thus have unique perspectives that can provide a more holistic view of the person's performance on various competencies.

While organizations started using the 360-degree feedback process mostly as a developmental tool, many companies are beginning to incorporate parts of the 360-degree process into their more formal performance appraisal systems. Philosophically, we support the use of data gathered from a 360-degree instrument, along with other objective measures. We do not support, however, replacing a more structured and objective performance appraisal solely with 360-degree feedback data. The 360-degree data serve as a tool to provide a more complete picture of overall performance and effectiveness, and they are most valuable when used in conjunction with other measures.

# WHAT IS THE TYPICAL METHODOLOGY USED FOR A 360-DEGREE FEEDBACK PROCESS?

Initially, 360-degree feedback was collected primarily through paper/pencil administration methods. Hard copies of surveys were distributed to raters in various rater groups, completed, and then submitted to our organization for data input and reporting. In the past 5 years, most organizations have transitioned to a more streamlined and cost-effective administration method—the Internet. Our organization has developed a proprietary application that enables participants and raters of a 360-degree process to easily access and complete their surveys via the Internet.

The participants and raters receive specific communication upfront about the value of the 360-degree process, roles and responsibilities, expectations, and so on.

Participants usually are involved at some level in selecting those individuals who will be asked to provide feedback. Once the individuals are identified, an e-mail is sent to each rater with specific instructions about how to access the online survey. Our process is completely confidential and anonymous for most rater groups. Typically, the responses imparted by the direct manager rater group are not anonymous and thus are identifiable in the report. This enables the direct manager to openly share his or her feedback and collaborate with the participant on the development of an action plan.

Raters usually have about 3 to 4 weeks to access the online system and respond to the survey. The typical response rate for our online administration is about 88 percent. Once all data have been submitted, the summary reports are processed and delivered to the participants. Most of those who participate in the process also take part in the feedback coaching sessions. This type of coaching enables the participant to further discuss the results with the assistance of a trained professional, who also helps the participant develop a meaningful action plan that will result in positive change.

# HOW DO WE KNOW THAT THE 360-DEGREE PROCESS RESULTS IN IMPROVEMENT?

Most of our clients participate in 360-degree assessments as an ongoing process, benchmarking and gauging their improvement in various areas over time. Over 93 percent of our clients who implement a 360-degree feedback process continue the process on a semiannual or annual basis. Many of the participants of this process also engage in a customized follow-up survey process, which enables them to solicit feedback on the two or three areas they have specifically targeted for improvement. This is a cost-effective, streamlined, and efficient way to determine whether positive change is actually occurring.

Our research has shown repeatedly that individuals who regularly follow up with their key stakeholders regarding their areas for development improve significantly as compared with those who do not. Figure A-1 represents aggregate results of overall leadership effectiveness from several organizations.

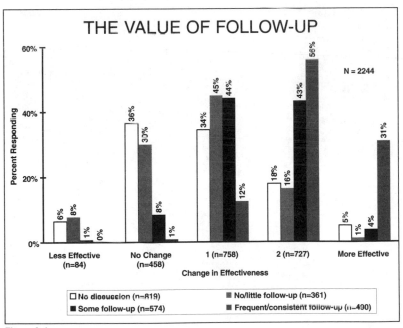

**Figure A-1**

Ninety-nine percent of leaders who consistently followed up improved at some level, with 87 percent achieving a +2 or +3 rating compared with 17 percent of leaders who did not follow up. Only 2 percent of leaders who followed up consistently or occasionally stayed the same or became less effective as compared to 38 percent of leaders who did not follow up.

Organizations are now beginning to conduct research that ties the improvement ratings of a 360-degree process to hard data, such as turnover rates, increased productivity, improved customer satisfaction ratings, and a general improvement in return on investment. Another important correlation is that of the 360-degree data as compared to the data collected from an organizational assessment that measures what employees think about a particular topic, such as their work environment, quality, or a company's business practices; when viewed together, it is common to see similarities in the overall scores within these two instruments. For example, *Transparency Edge 360*™ could be paired with an organizational assessment that measures how an organization's employees think about its company's transparency and credibility in business practices and management.

# Item Graphs

The following graphs show the results for a specific question or item from 360-degree assessments. These results, provided by Assessment Plus, were used to derive the statistics presented in this book. In deriving the statistics, I considered anything less than a rating of 4 or 5 as an indication that improvement could still be made. Leaders I have coached are not usually satisfied with assessment scores of 1–3, especially on items that measure such crucial behaviors of integrity and credibility.

Each graph, which is paired with the statistics presented in previous chapters, shows results by four rater groups: self, direct reports, peers, and manager. The first graph includes a key of explanation.

1. "In leadership assessments, over 50 percent of almost 13,000 peers and direct reports felt their leaders could improve in being honest and ethical" (see Chapter 2; see also Figure B-1).

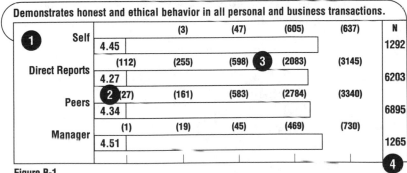

Figure B-1

1. **TITLE LINES.** These lines show results by rater group. In this example, responses from the participant's direct reports, peers, manager, and the participant (labeled as "Self") are shown.

2. **MEAN BAR.** The bars depict the average of the responses for each rating group.

3. **DISTRIBUTION.** The numbers in parentheses above each mean bar depict the number of responses provided for each point on the rating scale for that particular rater group.

4. **VALID N.** This column indicates the total number of raters in each group who responded to the item.

Various scales were used:

*Scale A* (most data use this scale):
    1 = significant improvement needed (or weakness)
    2 = slight improvement needed
    3 = skilled/competent
    4 = talented
    5 = role model

*Scale B:*
    1 = significant improvement needed
    2 = slight improvement needed
    3 = meets leadership competency
    4 = particularly talented
    5 = outstanding

*Scale C:*
    1 = highly dissatisfied
    2 = dissatisfied
    3 = neither satisfied nor dissatisfied
    4 = satisfied
    5 = highly satisfied

*Scale D:* The following 6-point scale was used on the item "Deals with issues in a candid manner (no hidden agendas)":

1 = unacceptable
2 = needs improvement
3 = developing skill
4 = competent
5 = talented
6 = role model

**2.** "In recent assessment surveys, only 26 percent of more than 4800 employees were highly satisfied with their leader's performance in communicating in a direct and straightforward manner" (see Chapter 2; see also Figure B-2).

| Communicates in a direct and straightforward manner. | | | | | | |
|---|---|---|---|---|---|---|
| | (6) | (73) | (212) | (218) | (75) | **N** |
| **Self** 3.49 | | | | | | 583 |
| **Direct Reports** | (42) | (191) | (436) | (668) | (579) | |
| 3.85 | | | | | | 1876 |
| **Peers** | (44) | (218) | (546) | (971) | (596) | |
| 3.78 | | | | | | 2375 |
| **Manager** | (19 | (60) | (143) | (241) | (92) | |
| 3.59 | | | | | | 555 |

Figure B-2

**3.** "In leadership surveys of 559 managers, 86 percent of 6023 of their followers and peers said that those leaders could improve at regularly asking for feedback" (see Chapter 3; see also Figure B-3).

| Regularly asks for feedback and suggestions to improve own performance. | | | | | | |
|---|---|---|---|---|---|---|
| **Self** | (9) | (125) | (129) | (241) | (55) | **N** |
| 3.37 | | | | | | 559 |
| **Direct Reports** | (131) | (502) | (443) | (1111) | (426) | |
| 3.46 | | | | | | 2613 |
| **Peers** | (69) | (595) | (694) | (1638) | (414) | |
| 3.51 | | | | | | 3410 |
| **Manager** | (3) | (39) | (143) | (355) | (99) | |
| 3.79 | | | | | | 639 |

Figure B-3

4. "In surveys, 95 percent of leaders were unable to give themselves the highest rating at demonstrating an understanding of their own strengths and weaknesses, and 98% of their bosses agreed" (see Chapter 3; see also Figure B-4).

**Demonstrates an understanding of his/her own strengths and weaknesses.**

| | | | | | | N |
|---|---|---|---|---|---|---|
| Self | (2) | (26) | (154) | (127) | (18) | |
| | 3.41 | | | | | 327 |
| Direct Reports | (27) | (90) | (325) | (437) | (316) | |
| | 3.77 | | | | | 1195 |
| Peers | (24) | (155) | (581) | (479) | (121) | |
| | 3.38 | | | | | 1360 |
| Manager | (12 | (41) | (188) | (103) | (6) | |
| | 3.14 | | | | | 350 |

Figure B-4

5. "Of 5612 executives, 79 percent said that their leaders could do better at promoting open and sincere communication" (see Chapter 3; see also Figure B-5).

**Promotes an environment of open and sincere communication.**

| | | | | | | N |
|---|---|---|---|---|---|---|
| Self | | (15) | (38) | (307) | (121) | |
| | 4.11 | | | | | 481 |
| Direct Reports | (176) | (446) | (245) | (977) | (703) | |
| | 3.62 | | | | | 2547 |
| Peers | (77) | (444) | (396) | (1646) | (502) | |
| | 3.67 | | | | | 3065 |
| Manager | | (24) | (70) | (295) | (132) | |
| | 4.03 | | | | | 521 |

Figure B-5

6. "Asked whether their leaders accept constructive feedback in a positive manner and without defensiveness, 76 percent of 7444 executives said that there is room for improvement, and 80 percent of those leaders' bosses agreed" (see Chapter 3; see also Figure B-6).

**Accepts constructive feedback from others in a positive manner (avoids defensiveness).**

| | | | | | | N |
|---|---|---|---|---|---|---|
| Self | (5) | (100) | (329) | (381) | (91) | |
| | 3.50 | | | | | 907 |
| Direct Reports | (130) | (316) | (750) | (1178) | (966) | |
| | 3.76 | | | | | 3340 |
| Peers | (82) | (406) | (1214) | (1595) | (807) | |
| | 3.64 | | | | | 4104 |
| Manager | (15) | (70) | (258) | (389) | (185) | |
| | 3.72 | | | | | 917 |

Figure B-6

**7.** "Out of 2052 employees who participated in surveys, 68 percent said that their leaders could improve at working constructively under pressure, and 73 percent of those leaders' bosses agreed" (see Chapter 4; see also Figure B-7).

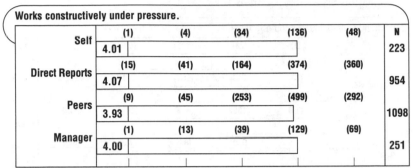

**Works constructively under pressure.**

| | (1) | (4) | (34) | (136) | (48) | N |
|---|---|---|---|---|---|---|
| Self 4.01 | | | | | | 223 |
| | (15) | (41) | (164) | (374) | (360) | |
| Direct Reports 4.07 | | | | | | 954 |
| | (9) | (45) | (253) | (499) | (292) | |
| Peers 3.93 | | | | | | 1098 |
| | (1) | (13) | (39) | (129) | (69) | |
| Manager 4.00 | | | | | | 251 |

Figure B-7

**8.** "When asked whether their boss displays a high degree of composure or emotional maturity, more than 60 percent of 2118 executives said that improvement was in order, and 73 percent of those leaders' bosses agreed" (see Chapter 4; see also Figure B-8).

**Shows a high degree of emotional maturity (e.g., composure, self-awareness).**

| | (3) | (8) | (51) | (122) | (40) | N |
|---|---|---|---|---|---|---|
| Self 3.84 | | | | | | 224 |
| | (18) | (43) | (154) | (308) | (462) | |
| Direct Reports 4.17 | | | | | | 985 |
| | (14) | (63) | (228) | (459) | (369) | |
| Peers 3.98 | | | | | | 1133 |
| | (4) | (22) | (35) | (123) | (69) | |
| Manager 3.91 | | | | | | 253 |

Figure B-8

**9.** "In surveys, more than half of 2197 people could not give their bosses the highest rating on being easy to talk to, and 76 percent of 1783 people said that their leaders were not entirely 'authentic'" (see Chapter 5; see also Figure B-9).

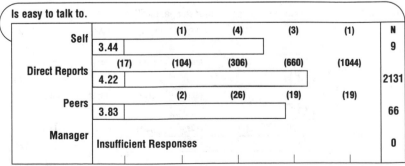

**Is easy to talk to.**

| | | (1) | (4) | (3) | (1) | N |
|---|---|---|---|---|---|---|
| Self 3.44 | | | | | | 9 |
| | (17) | (104) | (306) | (660) | (1044) | |
| Direct Reports 4.22 | | | | | | 2131 |
| | | (2) | (26) | (19) | (19) | |
| Peers 3.83 | | | | | | 66 |
| Manager | Insufficient Responses | | | | | 0 |

Figure B-9

10. "Of 12,000 employees, 55 percent believed that a boss or coworker could improve in consistently keeping promises. And of more than 1100 leaders, 67 percent admit they have room for improvement in promise-keeping" (see Chapter 6; see also Figure B-10).

**Consistently keeps his/her commitments.**

|  |  |  |  |  |  | N |
|---|---|---|---|---|---|---|
| Self | (1) | (28) | (125) | (609) | (368) |  |
|  | 4.16 |  |  |  |  | 1131 |
| Direct Reports | (75) | (249) | (686) | (2119) | (2720) |  |
|  | 4.22 |  |  |  |  | 5849 |
| Peers | (30) | (155) | (618) | (2638) | (2468) |  |
|  | 4.25 |  |  |  |  | 5909 |
| Manager |  | (22) | (86) | (456) | (549) |  |
|  | 4.38 |  |  |  |  | 1113 |

Figure B-10

11. "Of more than 1200 people surveyed in developmental assessments, 77 percent said that their leaders could improve at making realistic commitments" (see Chapter 6; see also Figure B-11).

**Makes realistic commitments (avoids over-committing).**

|  |  |  |  |  |  | N |
|---|---|---|---|---|---|---|
| Self | (2) | (29) | (27) | (22) | (6) |  |
|  | 3.01 |  |  |  |  | 86 |
| Direct Reports | (39) | (78) | (145) | (180) | (116) |  |
|  | 3.46 |  |  |  |  | 558 |
| Peers | (11) | (55) | (201) | (251) | (165) |  |
|  | 3.74 |  |  |  |  | 683 |
| Manager | (3) | (6) | (29) | (32) | (21) |  |
|  | 3.68 |  |  |  |  | 91 |

Figure B-11

12. "Of 1784 employees who participated in leadership assessments, 75 percent said that their leaders do not always deal with issues in a candid manner, and 72 percent of those leaders' peers agreed" (see Chapter 7; see also Figure B-12).

**Deals with issues in a candid manner (no "hidden agendas").**

|  |  |  |  |  |  |  | N |
|---|---|---|---|---|---|---|---|
| Self |  | (1) | (13) | (64) | (81) | (32) |  |
|  | 4.68 |  |  |  |  |  | 199 |
| Direct Reports | (9) | (47) | (69) | (189) | (276) | (276) |  |
|  | 4.74 |  |  |  |  |  | 829 |
| Peers | (6) | (43) | (82) | (272) | (353) | (162) |  |
|  | 4.53 |  |  |  |  |  | 954 |
| Manager | (2) | (2) | (13) | (734) | (66) | (45) |  |
|  | 4.66 |  |  |  |  |  | 426 |

Figure B-12

**13.** "In surveys, 91 percent of almost 1000 leaders said that they need to improve in effectively handling team members whose behavior undermines teamwork or partnerships. Of 8229 of those leaders' peers and direct reports, 79 percent agreed that there is work to be done" (see Chapter 7; see also Figure B-13).

**Effectively deals with individuals whose behavior undermines teamwork or partnerships.**

| | | | | | | N |
|---|---|---|---|---|---|---|
| **Self** | (16) | (115) | (324) | (430) | (88) | |
| | 3.47 | | | | | 973 |
| **Direct Reports** | (209) | (538) | (1049) | (1542) | (1029) | |
| | 3.61 | | | | | 4367 |
| **Peers** | (84) | (413) | (1202) | (1524) | (639) | |
| | 3.58 | | | | | 3863 |
| **Manager** | (19) | (74) | (232) | (460) | (161) | |
| | 3.71 | | | | | 945 |

Figure B-13

**14.** "In assessment surveys, 62 percent of leaders said that they could improve at admitting mistakes" (see Chapter 8; see also Figure B-14).

**Willingly admits his/her mistakes.**

| | | | | | | N |
|---|---|---|---|---|---|---|
| **Self** | | (5) | (27) | (201) | (143) | |
| | 4.28 | | | | | 376 |
| **Direct Reports** | (22) | (73) | (246) | (728) | (911) | |
| | 4.23 | | | | | 1980 |
| **Peers** | (5) | (39) | (232) | (892) | (610) | |
| | 4.16 | | | | | 1778 |
| **Manager** | | (2) | (19) | (179) | (171) | |
| | 4.40 | | | | | 371 |

Figure B-14

**15.** "In developmental assessments, 88 percent of leaders admitted that they could improve in avoiding destructive comments, and 83 percent of their bosses agreed" (see Chapter 9; see also Figure B-15).

**Avoids and discourages destructive comments about other people and organizations.**

| | | | | | | N |
|---|---|---|---|---|---|---|
| **Self** | (3) | (43) | (149) | (149) | (46) | |
| | 3.49 | | | | | 390 |
| **Direct Reports** | (36) | (93) | (269) | (590) | (725) | |
| | 4.09 | | | | | 1713 |
| **Peers** | (34) | (147) | (505) | (841) | (513) | |
| | 3.81 | | | | | 2040 |
| **Manager** | (7) | (32) | (111) | (112) | (47) | |
| | 3.52 | | | | | 309 |

Figure B-15

"In developmental surveys, 75 percent of leaders' peers said that improvement was in order in avoiding and discouraging destructive comments about other people and organizations, whereas only 58 percent of the same leaders' direct reports agreed" (see Chapter 9; see also Figure B-15).

16. "When asked whether their leaders demonstrate appreciation of others' concerns, feelings, motives, needs, and competencies, 79 percent of 7107 executives did not give their leaders the highest rating, and 91 percent of those executives' leaders actually agreed" (see Chapter 10; see also Figure B-16).

| Demonstrates appreciation of others' concerns, feelings, motives, needs, and competencies. | | | | | | |
|---|---|---|---|---|---|---|
| | (2) | (52) | (225) | (311) | (58) | N |
| Self 3.57 | | | | | | 648 |
| | (132) | (364) | (734) | (980) | (896) | |
| Direct Reports 3.69 | | | | | | 3106 |
| | (50) | (383) | (1399) | (1585) | (584) | |
| Peers 3.57 | | | | | | 4001 |
| | (5) | (46) | (249) | (274) | (60) | |
| Manager 3.53 | | | | | | 634 |

Figure B-16

212

# Index

# About the Authors

**Barbara Pagano, Ed.S.,** has coached more than 3,000 senior leaders and business owners to achieve lasting change in management behaviors for better results in organizations. As president of Executive Pathways, Pagano acts as an advisor, facilitator, and corporate leadership university faculty member to small businesses and Forture 100 companies like American Express, The Coca-Cola Company, AT&T, and Target.

**Elizabeth Pagano** has been an award-winning business reporter and columnist for a daily newspaper and numerous publications, covering a range of industries, decision-makers, and workplace issues of Fortune 500 corporations and small businesses. For more information, visit www.transparency edge.com.

To learn more about our consulting and coaching services and the instrument that measures leadership transparency and credibility, *Transparency Edge 360™*, please visit www.transparencyedge.com or reach us at:

**Executive Pathways**
Website: www.executivepathways.com
Email: info@executivepathways.com
Phone: 850-916-1129 or 888-865-0923

**Assessment Plus, Inc.**
Website: www.assessmentplus.com
Email: general@assessmentplus.com
Phone: 800-536-1470